THE MOST IMPORTANT BOOK

YOU WILL EVER READ

By
Jesus of Nazareth
&
Fr. Francis Pompei OFM

"You have only one Teacher."

"I will answer your questions about Life, Suffering, and Death. I will tell you what to do about them, how to do it, and then do it all with you."

DEDICATION

- *To all religions & Christian denominations.*
- *To all believers, atheists & agnostics.*
- *To the Poor & the Rich, the Young & the Old.*
- *To the oppressed, obsessed, or possessed by Evil.*
- *To those who suffer physically, mentally & emotionally.*
- *To the lonely, depressed & hopeless.*
- *To those looking for answers to the meaning of life.*
- *To those who fear death & the loss of loved ones.*
- *To children, born & unborn, who are abused.*
- *To families, torn apart by arguing, violence & war.*
- *To those who have lost their spiritual or moral compass.*
- *To my co-author, Jesus, who loves & believes in me, more than I do myself.*

...because Suffering, Death, Sin, and Fear are the common enemies to us all needing answers— regardless of religion, ideology, morality, age, or status.

LETTER BY THE EDITOR

Dear Reader,

It is my great privilege to have worked with the ever so wise & jubilant **Fr. Francis Pompei OFM** on this project. As you read, you will find that his intention tenderly seeps through with the loving guidance of our Lord Jesus Christ to lead you.

Here's my perspective on what his intention is in writing <u>THE MOST IMPORTANT BOOK YOU WILL EVER READ</u>. It's no small gesture.

I believe that the Catholic tradition, despite your faith or religion, is to be celebrated. It is the first Christian religion that has survived the test of time. For many, myself included, it is a foundation to begin the journey of a deep understanding of spirituality and devotion to God, the Universe, in all its glory. Despite the many scandals and criticisms of the Church—the truth, the core of it all remains the same. Jesus Christ is our Teacher, Brother and most importantly, our BEST FRIEND. He is and will always be (for anyone of the Christian faith) the ultimate example of Unconditional Love.

Fr. Pompei welcomes you to take a step back from all of life's chaos and look within. We already have all the tools we need. We can make it through whatever lesson and test, because, well... this life is the most important school you will ever attend. And this most important book you'll ever read reminds us that we are never alone, even when it feels like you're the last one on that important yellow school bus going Home.

So enjoy the ride! It is time to learn, to pray, and to play.

In Jesus' Unconditional Love,

Diandra Garcia

EDITOR

INTRODUCTION

Are you ready? I want to begin by telling you that one of the smartest things you did was buy this book. Why, you ask? You are finally going to get answers to most of your problems, fears, worries and suffering. In addition to this, you will learn what to do about them, and how. Now this should grab your attention right at the outset.

- ☐ As a Christian Catholic, I will be writing through the lens of a "believer."
- ☐ Those of you who are not believers are invited to read with a lens of Jesus of Nazareth's ideology— what He said, taught, and how He lived.

Here is more good news! Everything you will learn and do is not from some self-help book, a famous psychologist, evangelist, or guru, and especially not from me. My intention in writing this book is that everything, and I mean everything, that is contained in these pages comes from Jesus' ideology—what He said, what He taught, and how he lived. Now, you might say that Pastors, Imams, Rabbis, Theologians, and Evangelists have already done and are doing this, but the difference in this book is that Jesus Himself is going to give you specific answers, what to do, and how to do it, to all of the following:

QUESTIONS THAT NEED ANSWERS

- [ ] What is the meaning of your existence and life?
- [ ] Who and what are you?
- [ ] Why did God create you and send you here in these physical bodies?
- [ ] Why is there so much suffering?
- [ ] Why do little babies and children have to suffer and die? They are innocent!
- [ ] Why do you have to watch your loved ones die?
- [ ] Why is there so much violence in the world, wars, terrorism, rape, murder, sex abuse, drugs, addiction, human trafficking, beheadings, bullying, shootings, and mental abuse?
- [ ] Why is there so much hatred, arguing, retaliation, and division, and why isn't Jesus doing something about it if He really loves us?
- [ ] Why do some people suffer more than others do?
- [ ] I pray and go to church, but it seems like God does not hear, and it seems to only get worse.
- [ ] What is this emptiness and void in me, that no possession, person, or activity seems to fill or satisfy completely?
- [ ] Jesus said, "Don't be afraid or let your hearts be troubled (Worry)." I've asked Him a million times to help me, but when I finish and say *Amen*, I am still frightened and worried.
- [ ] What about people who hurt me and are not interested in forgiveness? Why should I forgive them?
- [ ] Jesus said I should forgive my enemies. I'm supposed to forgive a rapist, terrorist, murderer, sex abuser, drug dealer, trafficker of young kids and women. I don't think so. They deserve what they get.
- [ ] The last sentence in the Our Father is "deliver us from Evil." I pray it all the time, but why does God allow Evil to still attack, tempt, seduce and overwhelm me with guilt and self-hatred.
- [ ] If I am to do God's Will, how do I know what His will is when I don't hear Him? How can I do His will if He doesn't reveal it to me?
- [ ] Does God really communicate with us, or is this another mystery I have to accept?
- [ ] If Jesus came into the world to conquer Evil and save us from Sin, Suffering, and Death, where is it?

This is the reason why many, if not most people leave the Church or religion all together. I cannot blame them. If there are no changes when it comes to Sin, Suffering, and Death since this Jew named Jesus came 2000 years ago, then why would, or should, anybody believe in Him as the Son of God and the Savior of the world? Makes sense to me!

Wouldn't it be great to get answers to all of the above? Well, here they are, according to Jesus Himself. Fasten your spiritual seatbelt, hold tight, and let's GO!

THE PURPOSE OF THIS BOOK BEFORE YOU START

Jesus is personally going to give you not only the answers to your questions about Life, Suffering, and Death listed in the Introduction, but teach you **What to do** about them and How to do it. He will give you opportunities to retrain your mind, experience forgiveness, healing, deliverance, joy, and the peace He promised.

- ☐ Wouldn't it be great to know who and what you are, and God's plan for you?
- ☐ Wouldn't it be great to be able to experience and say what St. Paul did near the end of his life?

"It is no longer I who live, but Christ Jesus, my Lord, who lives in me."
(Gal. 2:20)

Lastly, the best part is that Jesus will be right there with you as your Teacher and friend, journeying with you, transforming you from being a believer to His "Disciple" and "Brother."

*JESUS:

When you see Jesus' name capitalized and underlined, His words and teachings are what follows, as well as the Word of God. *(Scripture)*

LIFE IS SCHOOL, AND THIS WILL BE YOUR

- **TEXT BOOK**
  For your life here, in these physical bodies

- **HOMEWORK**
  To put on the Mind of Christ

- **MEDITATION AND PRAYER BOOK**
  To communicate with the Lord

- **TRAINING TO CONQUER FEAR OF SUFFERING AND DEATH**
  To deliver yourself from Fear

- **STRESS MANAGEMENT**
  Limits and boundaries to set you free

- **PLAN BOOK FOR MARRIAGE, FAMILY, AND CHURCH**
  Loving one another

- **DELIVERANCE FROM EVIL MANUAL**
  Attacking Evil, Temptation, and Sin

- **DISCERNMENT OF GOD'S WILL**
  Your daily adventure with Jesus

- **TRAINING PROGRAM FOR THE UNCONDITIONAL**
  Love, Forgiveness, and Generosity

TABLE OF CONTENTS

CHAPTER 1:
WHO AND WHAT YOU ARE

"God created man in His own image and likeness." (Gen. 1:27)

Here is your first answer... perhaps one you already knew and even believed in. But have you ever experienced it as the truth about yourself?

WHAT ARE YOU?

BRAIN: Physical receiver of the sensory transmissions

MIND: Non-physical converter from physical reality to non-physical thoughts, images, emotions, feelings, desires, memory, and **conscience**

SENSES: Physical receptors transmitted to the brain

CONSCIENCE is the non-physical power of the mind that has been described in many ways—an inner voice, a moral compass of what is right and wrong. It has also been described as a guide and reminder of what behaviors are meaningful to us.

The power of **conscience** is part of our mind and needs to be developed; otherwise, it remains dormant. An example is when we hear a group of young men beating a young woman and leaving her for dead, showing no remorse, sense of guilt, or responsibility. Psychologists, lawyers, and judges may refer to them as "cold as steel" having no conscience. What this means is they have an underdeveloped conscience.

So what is a **conscience** and how does it work? How do we develop a healthy one?

A HEALTHY CONSCIENCE

1. **WARNS:** You **SHOULD NOT** do this.

2. **JUDGES:** This is **WRONG**.

3. **BLAMES:** You are **GUILTY**.

EXAMPLE:

A teenage girl gets permission from her parents to go to a dance but has to go home right after it ends. On the way, she runs into some of her friends who tell her, "No one is going to the dance." A classmate is having a party at his house, and the parents are away. The teenager says No at first, because it (her conscience) **WARNS** her that she should not, but after a lot of coaxing, she chooses to go.

While at the party, someone offers her a beer. Her conscience once again WARNS that she should not, but she ends up drinking it. Now, she is having a grand ol' time when her conscience keeps interrupting with **JUDGMENT**: "What you are doing is **WRONG**."

Lastly, feelings of guilt, shame, and fear enter and begin to take over her mind. Her conscience is **BLAMING** her, and this takes away the pleasure and fun out of the party. What makes it worse is that when it is finished, there is no more partying, friends or beer. She feels disappointed in herself and wants to hide what she has done.

Now you know what a **CONSCIENCE** is and how it operates. If you take this knowledge and apply it to the story of the young men who attacked the woman and showed no remorse or responsibility, now you know why. Their consciences were underdeveloped. It did not **WARN, JUDGE,** or **BLAME**.

HOW TO DEVELOP A CONSCIENCE:

Knowing and learning what makes certain ways of thinking and behaviors right or wrong

RIGHT: determined by Natural Law and Objective Truth. Your thoughts and actions will affect you, others, and society in the present and in the future.

EXAMPLE: If someone throws a rock at you, you instinctively try to block and avoid it. This is our nature—to protect ourselves from harm and death. Life and existence wants to continue to exist and not end. Therefore, this is Natural Law telling us that to preserve life is **RIGHT**, and to kill or destroy someone is **WRONG**.

To determine what is **Right** and **Wrong**, like in the case of the teenager who chose to go the party instead of the dance and have a couple beers, we could ask ourselves how will it benefit us, our relationship with our parents, and our future being a trustworthy person as a husband, wife, father, or mother? In addition to this, how will it affect the local community and society as a whole?

WILL: Our ability to discern and choose between Good and Evil;

truth and deception; action and inaction; to choose what we download into our minds or reject so as to prevent negative, half-truths and lies from affecting or infecting our decision-making and behavior.

<u>CONSCIOUSNESS</u>: Pure nonphysical self-awareness; our spiritual nature and self; our unique person or soul; the self that knows and is aware of what is in the mind. This includes the feelings, emotions, and desires that enter the mind through senses, thoughts and images.

<u>EXERCISE</u>: EXPERIENCE WHO AND WHAT YOU ARE

Step 1: Mark this page, close the book, stare at the cover and memorize it for 10 seconds.

Step 2: Close your eyes and picture it in your mind for 10 seconds.

Step 3: Can you see the book in your mind?

Step 4: Yes is your answer.

If I had a scalpel and opened your brain, would I find the book in it? No, because the book is in your mind, is not physical, and therefore is somewhere *in* you, because you can see it. That place is your **MIND**, which is not physical. **Get it!**

So, too, if I ask you to remember the image again, you could, because the electrical impulses from your senses have transported it to a certain part of your brain where information is stored. But like a computer file, it needs to be opened up to see what is in it. **Bingo!** That is your **MIND** that opens it up.

Then there is the sheer bliss you are experiencing from just seeing my book, and you are overwhelmed with joy. Put some electrodes on your brain and the sound waves go off the charts. You experience perfect joy at the image of my book, because your **MIND** opens up the waves.

Stay with me, because all this is necessary for two reasons:

1. You will finally know who and what you really are.

2. You will not only be able to understand all the answers to your questions in this book and introduction, but you will know what to do about them and how.

Sounds like pretty good gifts the Lord has given us, right?

EXERCISE: EXPERIENCE YOUR WILL

"Maybe I will, maybe I won't." Your **WILL**, which is also non-physical, is the power to reflect and choose between this or that.

Reality enters through your senses, then your **MIND** opens it up. Next, you reflect on those things that require a choice or action. Your **CONSCIENCE** (memory, future projections, pros and cons) influences your decision. Finally, you choose to act or not, download it or not, and to think about it or not.

This is your **WILL** in action.

EXERCISE: EXPERIENCE YOUR CONSCIOUSNESS

Let's go back to the image of the book that's probably still in your MIND.

The next question is the most important one. Who is "seeing" the book? In your response you said, "**I** can see the book." **Bingo again!** That **I** that you use a thousand times a day is your **CONSCIOUSNESS**, your unique person and awareness that is YOU. In religious circles, because your consciousness is not physical, this is referred to as your Spirit or Soul.

What does all this have to do with God, faith and answers to all the problems in your life? NOTHING!

I'm only kidding. It has everything to do with them. Isn't it good to finally know who and what you are? Isn't it good, once and for all, to know that the God who created you in His/Her own image unconditionally loves you? And isn't it beyond words to know that you and I – our **CONSCIOUSNESS, MIND,** and **WILL** – are ultimately **not physical**? Therefore, we are not subject to death and will live forever! Alleluia!

Now that you know who and what you are and all the powers that make you, let's jump into our next chapter. Be aware that Jesus (not me) is the Author and your Teacher giving you all the answers to your questions—the Truth. Alleluia, again!

CHAPTER 2:
LIFE IS SCHOOL, DEATH IS GRADUATION

"You have only one Teacher,

The Holy Spirit, Who will teach you everything." *(Jn. 14:26)*

JESUS:

"When I said that I am with you every day until the end of time, I meant it. But the world and life is so complex and over-stimulating that it holds and possesses your attention. That is why you are overwhelmed with problems, confusion, fear, and suffering. This is how the world has trained you to think and live. I came to teach and show you another way, to become aware of me with and in you, throughout your day. The more you do this; the less and less you will be afraid of your problems and suffering, because you will be aware that I am with you. And together WE will deal with them. You will learn to leave all the fear and worrying up to me, instead of trying to be in control and fix everything yourself.

This is why I came into the world, to transform the way you think and offer you an intimate journey with me every day. So keep reading, pay attention, and learn from me. Do not just believe in Me. Instead, become my disciple, brother, sister and friend. Most of all, remember that I believe in you. I am counting on you and love you...always have...always will. Amen!"

You have heard it said or probably said it yourself, that "Life is Hell." My guess is that all of us have felt this way at some time or another, because of all the suffering and death in the world, from the beginning of humankind. To put it simply, somehow superior beings, fallen angels *(according to Scripture)* or other conscious beings with divine knowledge rebelled against God, chose physical reality, lusted after human women *(Forbidden fruit)* and interfered with our DNA. This affected our physical minds and bodies as well all physical reality. Evil's origins will be discussed in more detail in later chapters.

"All creation groans for the salvation of the Lord." *(Rom. 8:19-23)*

The logical conclusion from the opening Scripture of this chapter is that we must be in school and Jesus is our Teacher. This is not an analogy, but the truth according to Jesus and the Holy Spirit who will teach us all things.

So God created our Consciousness, Mind, and Will in Heaven *(The Spirit World)*. Then He sent and bonded us with the physical bodies that our parents co-created with God, but to do what? Why couldn't we stay in Heaven and be perfectly happy, instead of being in these bodies that suffer and die? What do we need to go to school for?

THE ANSWER: To learn and grow. We can learn and grow more here than we can in Heaven or the Spirit World. Why? Because there is both Good and Evil, Sin, Suffering, Fear, Loneliness, and then Death... All of these require making decisions. By paying attention to the Teacher *(Jesus and the Holy Spirit)*, we learn what to do and how to do it to become all that we were created to be.

Let me put some reality on this. We spent the first five or six years of our existence attached to our mothers/caregivers all day every day. They packed our lunch one day, put us on a strange bus with a strange driver with 30 strange kids, and then went to a strange building. **And Mommy didn't come with us.** What kind of mother would do that to their child?

Then it got worse. We were marched into a room with 20 more strange kids and a strange person that was not Mommy but called "Teacher." Worst of all is that Mommy left us there alone for almost 6 hours. No wonder some kids were hitting the teacher, screaming for Mommy, and punching each other. I thought that Mommy loved me. If she really loved me, why did she send me to **HELL!**

Is this starting to make sense to you? **LIFE IS NOT HELL. LIFE IS SCHOOL.** For the same reason that our parents sent us to school, to learn how to make our own decisions between Good and Evil, right and wrong, respect, values, relationships, and the life skills to deal with problems, anger, suffering, and fear.

SUMMARY: Now we know who we are and why God sent us here and bonded us with the physical bodies our parents produced. That is— **to go to school.** Everything that you and I experience while we are in these physical bodies is being in school. As long as our bodies exist, we are still in school. **Therefore, life is school, and all that happened is happening and will happen** (good or bad) **is an OPPORTUNITY TO LEARN.**

☐ **Memorize this last sentence.**

From now on, for the rest of your earthly life, say it to the Lord at the beginning of your day, and the moment you are facing a problem. Be open to learn whatever it is, good or bad.

This is the new paradigm or context that you need to discern and measure everything with. The real truth is that **Life is School** and this will dispel all the confusion, frustration, and temptations to doubt God.

Now you will know who and what you are, and why you are here. This is great news, if you ask me. After the initial shock of Mommy abandoning you when she sent you to Kindergarten, you gradually adjusted to the strangeness and strangers by listening to the teacher, and you were no longer afraid but actually wanted to go to school and learn. Makes sense to me!

The following chart will explain what life is about in the context of being in school and what God wants us to learn while we are here.

LIFE IS NOT HELL, LIFE IS SCHOOL

THE SCHOOL BUILDING	**OUR PHYSICAL BODIES** God bonds our Consciousness, Mind & Will with our physical bodies that our parents produced. The same reason our mothers sent us to school.
THE DEGREE WE ARE TO GRADUATE WITH	**TRUST: TRUST IN GOD** is the reason we are in school, not to be "perfect." *"Thy will be done"* (Mt. 6:10) *"Trust in God"* (Jn. 14:1) No matter what we think or feel with our Will, choose to let go of control and **TRUST.** *(Do it the Lord's way.)*

SUBJECTS TO GROW IN EVERY DAY	**UNCONDITIONAL** ☐ **LOVE:** "Love God with your whole heart, mind, and soul." *(Mt. 22:37)* ☐ **GENEROSITY:** "The Blessings you have received, give them freely. I was hungry and you gave me something to eat…" *(Mt. 25)* ☐ **FORGIVENESS:** "Love your enemies," "Forgive us our trespasses, as we forgive those who trespass against us." *(Lk. 6:35)*
TEACHER	**JESUS: "You have only one Teacher. The Holy Spirit will teach you all things."** *(Jn. 14:26) Learn to think like Jesus and live like Jesus.*
	"Do not conform yourself to this World but put on the mind of Christ." This requires working on this 24-7, as long as we are in these bodies. (School)
BEING A GOOD STUDENT	**PAY ATTENTION- Train** your brain. If you don't, You won't learn. Focus on Jesus, and not the problem, lies, negative thoughts, half-truths. If you do not discipline and train your mind to do this, it's like looking out the window in school. You won't learn what to do or how to do deal with your problems or suffering. Then fear will take over. ☐ **"You cannot serve God and money."** *(Mt. 6:24) (Power/Pleasure/Sports)* ☐ **"If anyone would be my disciple, you must DENY your very selves, pick up your cross, and follow me."** *(Lk. 9:23)*

DAILY HOMEWORK, EXERCISES DRILLS	**SACRIFICING FOR OTHERS** ☐ To learn God's way of thinking and living through acts of love, generosity, forgiveness, sacrificing what you want or want to do, for the sake of others— It's called **LOVE.**
POP QUIZZES	<u>**SMALL PROBLEMS**</u>: <u>**OPPORTUNITIES**</u> to learn how to Trust by doing it. **"If you TRUST me in small things, I will place you over greater."** *(Lk. 16:10)*
TESTS	**ARE THE MORE SERIOUS PROBLEMS AND SUFFERING:** <u>**OPPORTUNITIES**</u> to learn how to deal with Fear-Worry-Doubt by trusting in Jesus. **"Nothing can separate us from the love of God in Christ Jesus my Lord, for in all things we are more than conquerors."** *(Rom. 8:31)*
RECESS	**IS WHEN THINGS ARE GOING WELL, AND YOU ARE AT PEACE,** because you are learning how to deal with problems, fear, and suffering, together with Jesus.
	"I have come to give you Peace of Mind and give you JOY and make your experience of joy complete." *(Jn. 14:27)*
VACATION	**LONGER PERIODS OF PEACE** This is the result of your trusting the Lord, and becoming aware of Him, more and more when dealing with life and living His way. This is a foretaste of Heaven. Get ready for **EXAMS**. Then move up a grade! **Hooray!**

FINAL EXAMS DYING	GRADUATION: Your Consciousness, Mind, Will, (your Soul—You are non-physical, remember?) leaves your body (school building) and goes to your real home, where God created you. Death is graduation and commencement, Heaven/ eternal life. No more Suffering, Evil, or Death. Alleluia! **You did it!**

DEATH IS GRADUATION ACCORDING TO JESUS

- ☐ *"Our citizenship is in Heaven." (Phil. 3:20)*
- ☐ *"Unless the seed falls to the ground and dies, it remains just a seed, but if it falls to the ground and dies, it will bear much fruit." (Jn. 12:24)*
- ☐ *"I am the resurrection and life. Anyone who believes in me, when your physical body dies, I will raise you up. (Your Soul, Consciousness, Mind, and Will that I created, to come back home with me forever) (Jn. 11:17)*
- ☐ *"Therefore we do not lose heart, but though our outer body is decaying, our inner spirit is being renewed day by day. For our suffering and affliction is TEMPORARY (School) and producing for us an eternal HOME (Graduation-New Life), and a glory far beyond all comparison. So, while we do not look at the things which are seen (Things of the world and physical reality- pleasure, entertainment, power, money, possessions, etc.) but at the things **which are not seen (Jesus With/In Us)**. For the things which are seen are temporal and passing away, but the things which are not seen, are eternal." (2 Cor. 4:18)*
- · **EXERCISE: Burn the above words** into your minds and replace Evil's lies.

ASSIGNMENT: **Memorize them!** Remember you are in school, so do not look out the window. Stop reading this book, memorize these Scriptures, and replace the half-truths, lies, and negative thoughts that you have downloaded and infected that mind of yours with. **DO IT!**

There is more great news and Truth to come on the subject of Death and Resurrection later in the **Chapter on DEATH.**

CHAPTER 3:
THE HOLY SPIRIT, OR YOU ARE WASTING YOUR TIME

Many Christians, especially Catholics, have never experienced the Holy Spirit and the unconditional love of Jesus. Without judging anyone or the Church, I believe this is true, because in the past no one ever taught us that we could experience the Holy Spirit or even "How to." This experience of intimacy with God is missing in many of the leaders in faithful parish communities. The most tragic thing is that this is the whole purpose of the coming of Jesus, His Life, Suffering, Death and Resurrection.

Specifically, this was and is the ultimate goal of God and not my own interpretation. Listen to Jesus' words and prayer, just before His Passion and Death.

JESUS:

*"I am praying not only for these disciples, but also for all who will believe in me through their message. **I pray that they will all be one, just as you and I are one, as you are in me, Father, and I am in you. May they be one in us. By the love they have for one another, the world will believe you sent me.***

I have given them the glory you gave me, so they may be one, as we are one.** May they experience such perfect oneness that the world will know that you sent me, **that you love them as much as you love me." (Jn. 17:21)

This intimacy and oneness with God, through Jesus, is God the Holy Spirit. It was God's Unconditional Love for us, driving Jesus to experience, endure, and overcome the fear of Death and Suffering.

STOP READING: Take a moment to imagine Jesus on the cross, frightened and dying yet moment by moment choosing to experience his horrific suffering and immanent death...

Then ask Him to embrace you with the love He has for you that is driving Him to endure it...

Close your eyes, and imagine yourself experiencing it.

SUMMARY:

- ☐ Jesus saves us from Evil, our fear of Suffering and Death, and forgives our sins.
- ☐ The Holy Spirit is the restoration of the intimacy with God that was lost because of Evil and Original Sin

SCRIPTURE:

"When the day of Pentecost came, they were all together in one place. Suddenly a sound like the blowing of a violent wind came from Heaven and filled the whole house where they were sitting. They saw what seemed to be tongues of fire that separated and came to rest on each of them. **All of them were filled with the Holy Spirit** *and began to speak in other tongues, as the Spirit enabled them." (Acts 2:1)*

EXPLAINED IN REAL LIFE TERMS

The followers of Jesus in the upper room at Pentecost felt the unconditional love of God for the first time among each other, just as Jesus prayed for in John's gospel.

What is this like? It is exactly like the unconditional love of a mother for her child through her embrace. There is peace, comfort, and love.

Remember how unbelievably wonderful this was with our mother, grandmother, father, or guardian? When you experience God's unconditional love, there are no words to describe how complete and fulfilled you are. Nothing here on Earth can compare or come close to it. God not only created us, but He also created us for Himself. That is why no thing, person, or activity here, while we are in our earthly bodies, can ever satisfy us completely.

Only becoming one with God's love will. This is why some Christians, who have experienced the Holy Spirit say they have been "saved," and ask others if they have been saved. What they are saying is, "Have you experienced intimacy with Jesus Christ through the Holy Spirit?"

A PERSONAL RELATIONSHIP WITH JESUS

Listen carefully and pay attention. Intimacy with the Lord is not the end but just the beginning. It is the beginning of experiencing not only the love of God as a "warm fuzzy," "moon struck," and "volcanic" eruption of passion and joy, but it is meant to refocus our attention from "looking out the window" to the world for fulfillment and focusing instead on who and what we were created for—God.

After we experience the Lord and Baptism of the Holy Spirit, we want to experience and "**know**" Him more and more. What we are talking about here is establishing a deep, personal relationship with Jesus. I want to say it again—**a deep and personal relationship** with Jesus.

Here is where many Christians, especially Catholics, get confused. Now, don't send me any messages, saying that I am picking on Catholics. I am a Catholic and proud of it. I am just speaking from my general experience where a significant number of Catholics seem to have mostly a <u>monologue</u> relationship with Jesus. In other words, they are baptized, make their First Penance and Communion, get confirmed, go to mass, say the rosary and *recite prayers*.

This is good and inspiring but is only a faith relationship based upon a **monologue**. Those who pray this way do all the talking and seldom listen to Jesus talking to them—to know His will. Jesus also helps make tough decisions, heals, forgives, and delivers us from fear and worry.

The kind of relationship Jesus wants with you and me is a **dialogue**. How do I know this is His Will and not my interpretation or teaching? I'll let Jesus teach you Himself.

JESUS:

- *"While you are in the world you will suffer, but don't be afraid, for **I am with you** until the end of time." (Jn. 16:33)*
- *"Come to me all who labor and are heavy burdened, and **I will give you rest.**" (Mt. 28)*
- *"Who is my mother, father, brothers and sisters? **It is the one who hears and does the will of my Father.**" (Mt. 12)*
- *"I have come **to give you life** and life to the fullest." (Jn. 10:10)*

23

☐ *"I have come **to give you joy** and make your joy complete." (Jn. 15:11)*
☐ *"So, do not be afraid or let your hearts be troubled. **Trust in God and trust in me."** (Jn. 14:1)*

EXERCISE: Read each one of Jesus' words again, twice, imagining that He is right there with you saying them, **because He is.** When you finish, there is some good news.

You have just heard Jesus speaking to you... and maybe for the first time.

ALLELUIA!

Congratulations, you are on your way and just entered Kindergarten. But you are finally in SCHOOL and paying attention to your Teacher.

GOOD NEWS! YOU ARE NOT ALONE

☐ For God so loved the world that he gave his one and only Son, that whoever believes in him shall not perish but have eternal life. *(Jn. 3:16)*

The key word is **World**. God did not just save you but the whole world. If salvation is experiencing forgiveness, unconditional love, and a personal relationship with Jesus, then one of His greatest guidelines is to feel His presence whenever we are together with others who love Him.

☐ *"Wherever two or three are gathered in my Name, I will be there in their midst." (Mt. 18:20)*
☐ *"They went to the temple area together **every day**. While in their homes they broke bread, **prayed** and took their meals together. And the place where they prayed **shook**, as they were all **filled with the Holy Spirit** and continued to **witness** to Jesus, with boldness, **and their numbers increased."** (Acts 5:42)*

- "I want you to love one another, as I have loved you." (Jn. 13:34)
- "By the way you love one another, the world will know that the Father sent me." (Jn. 13:35)

SUMMARY

- The way the Lord can communicate with us is through an intimate personal relationship. In addition to this, we can feel His presence when we gather with others who have experienced Him and have the same relationship with Him.
- At the last supper, Jesus said, "I do not think of you as my servants, but I call you my <u>friends</u>. Whoa! Is Jesus kidding us? You mean to tell me that God, the Creator of the whole ball of wax, you and me included, is our Friend? Wow! It's unbelievable.
- Jesus is telling us the kind of relationship God wants with us; that is, one of friendship. He is telling us how He wants to be treated. Yea, Yea, Yea, He wants to be acknowledged as our Lord, and rightly so, but also as our Friend.
- In other words, be yourself, trust Him, and talk to Him as you would your best friend.

What to do and the way to do this is coming up next. Thank you, Jesus!

TRUST
The Way To Answers

A mother of two teenagers once told me, "It isn't enough to just believe, go to church, receive Communion, say prayers and try to lead a good life. You need to experience Jesus, the Baptism of the Holy Spirit, and have a personal relationship with Him."

I have heard this millions and millions of times from people—even children to senior citizens—who have felt the awesome love of Jesus for and in them. They are people who went to church, have been faithful and believe. So, what are they saying that happened to them, and how is Jesus transforming their lives?

Through a personal dialogue relationship with Jesus every day, all day, now the Lord can teach you, forgive you, heal you, and help you with your decision-making by a deep awareness that He is actually with you as He said. *("I will be with you every day")* Whoa! You mean to tell me that I've been dealing with my problems, fears, worries and suffering alone, saying "Help me Lord" prayers and trying to fix them by myself feeling as if He isn't hearing me from a million miles away?

Being baptized by the Holy Spirit is essential in having a personal relationship with Jesus. This is the way we establish a friendship with anybody. We need to know them first, and that is by spending time with them and experiencing them, not just receiving information about them.

The question here that Jesus and I want to answer is, what is the Baptism of the Holy Spirit?

THE BAPTISM OF THE HOLY SPIRIT

<u>WHAT IS IT?</u>

- ☐ When baptized with the Holy Spirit, you will receive an intimate embrace and experience of the Lord's unconditional love.
- ☐ **You will experience a new strength and boldness** from God, to overcome temptation, Evil, and <u>Sin</u>.
- ☐ You will know when you have experienced the Baptism of the Holy Spirit, because it is unlike anything else you have felt with your faith. The apostles at Pentecost experienced the Holy Spirit like a strong driving wind and fire.

<u>PETER AND CORNELIUS</u> *(A Roman Centurion)* and his whole household experienced the Holy Spirit and praised the Lord in tongues.

"Peter went inside and found a large gathering of people. He said to them: 'You are well aware that it is against our law for a Jew to associate with or visit a Gentile. However, God has shown me that I should not call anyone impure or unclean. Why have you sent for me?'

'Now we are all here in the presence of God to listen to everything the Lord has commanded you, Peter, to tell us.'

Then Peter began to speak: 'We are witnesses of everything Jesus did in the country of the Jews and in Jerusalem. They killed him by hanging him on a cross, but God raised him from the dead on the third day and caused Him to be seen by us. He commanded us to preach to the people and testify that He is the one whom God appointed as Judge of the living and the dead.

While Peter was still speaking these words, the Holy Spirit came on all who heard the message. The circumcised believers who arrived with Peter were astonished that the Holy Spirit was poured out upon the Gentiles, because they heard them speaking in tongues and praising God.

Then Peter said, Surely no one can stand in the way of their being baptized with water. They have received the Holy Spirit, just as we have.' Peter ordered they be baptized with water in the name of Jesus Christ. *(Acts 10)*

THE EXPERIENCE OF THE HOLY SPIRIT

- ☐ Your life is changed. God's power often passes through your body like a powerful current and fills you with an infinite joy and happiness.
- ☐ The apostles were so full of joy that the people thought they were drunk.
- ☐ There is no set timetable for when you experience the Baptism of the Holy Spirit.

IMPORTANT

How each of us experiences the Holy Spirit differs according to where we are in our relationship with God and Jesus Christ. Some experience the Baptism like the apostles at Pentecost and Cornelius' family, while others more gradually through preachers, teachers, witnesses, and situations. Others who are filled with the Spirit can be made evident just by looking at them.

It's like what Jesus said to Nicodemus, the Pharisee: "The Spirit is like the Wind. You cannot see it, yet it moves where it will and when it will."

Some denominations preach that you are "not saved" unless you experience the Holy Spirit exactly the way they did at Pentecost. As Catholics, we don't believe that is the only way the Spirit moves or saves.

- *"Anyone who believes in their heart and confesses with their lips that Jesus Christ is Lord will be saved." (Rom. 10:9)*
- *"God is love, and anyone who loves, knows God. God is in them and they are in God." (1 Jn. 4:16)*
- *"Enter into the kingdom prepared for you from the beginning of time, for I was hungry, and you gave me something to eat; thirsty and you gave me a drink..." (Mt. 25)*

WHY YOU NEED THE BAPTISM OF THE HOLY SPIRIT

- When baptized with the Holy Spirit, you will become bold and unafraid, just as Peter, the Blessed Mother, and Jesus' followers were on the day of Pentecost.
- The Word of the God will suddenly become alive for you, and you will experience wisdom and guidance from God's word, especially when you come into difficult situations.
- You will be less afraid of anyone or anything, not even Evil itself by living every day for the Lord.
- You will receive gifts of the Holy Spirit, according to the Lord's plan for your life and service: Healing, Preaching, Witnessing boldly, Teaching, Discernment of the Lord's Will, and Spiritual Works of Mercy.

TEENS' WITNESS COMMENTS

- "I only wish I experienced Jesus before, when I was a kid. Jesus is great, and He is 'big time' in my life now." *(Jason, Florida)*
- "When I first experienced Jesus, it is hard to describe, because. I mean, He's God and all, but it was incredible. He really loves me and believes in me." *(Maggie, NJ)*
- "A lot of kids at school think it is '**un-cool**,' to believe in

Jesus, go to church, and pray. Boy, are they missing out. I feel sorry for them." *(Jim, NJ)*

☐ "Now when I go to mass, I'm not bored, because I go to spend time with and talk to Jesus, and many times I can feel him right there, especially when I go to Communion." *(Dan, NH)*

☐ "I am in a teenage prayer group, and we pray together at Youth Group. One of my best friends, that I have been friends with since the first grade, is not in my prayer group. I have been going to the prayer group for only two years, and I feel closer to them than I do with my friend from first grade. I think the reason is we pray and have actually experienced Jesus together."

(Mike, Buffalo, NY)

☐ "If I could, I would tell every teenager and adult that Jesus wants them to experience the Holy Spirit and is waiting for them to ask. I have experienced Jesus and have a personal relationship with him now. He's more of a friend now and not like what a lot of people and even I use to do— just go to church, listen to stories about Jesus, and say prayers to Him. Now I want to go to church and get involved in Ministry and Service and live the way Jesus wants me to. The joy and peace I have experienced is greater than anything other kids who don't believe in Jesus have offered me in high school." *(Hannah, NY)*

If all we do is believe, go to church, say prayers, and try to lead a good life, we are missing the **"more"** of why God came in Jesus—the Baptism of the Holy Spirit.

"Wait here for the fulfillment of my Father's promise, the Holy Spirit, who will teach you all things." (Lk. 24:49)

That is why many Christians do not experience the Lord with them, His strength, love, or wisdom. If you have not, don't get down on yourself and feel like you have done something wrong. The reason you are not experiencing the Lord is not because of something you have done wrong. The Lord is with you and loves you. It is because nobody taught you what to do and how to do it. **So get ready for the most important answer, not only to this question, but also to the heart and soul of everything that this book is about... how to experience the Lord.**

THE ANSWER

Here is a quick pop quiz to see if you have been paying attention.

"If Life is School, do you remember what degree we are to graduate with?"

A degree in _____ ?

If you had to look back at the chart, you cheated. If you got the answer, then you are in the second semester of kindergarten. **Congratulations!**

The Lord is teaching you that **TRUST** is the key that unlocks the door to everything the Lord wants us to know and experience.

CHAPTER 4:
"TRUST IN GOD & TRUST IN ME" FINALLY, HOW TO DO IT

TRUST

THAT'S RIGHT. IT'S TRUST. We need to know the difference between **Faith** and **Trust**. The difference is this.

FAITH is **WHAT** you believe. It is in the mind, thoughts, truths, theology, and beliefs. *(Example: The Apostles' Creed)* Faith is our great gift from God, but to know God, and I mean really know Him and His love, is not with information, theology, commandments, or stories about Him. It is through **TRUST** that we know Him, by experiencing and becoming intimately one with Him.

Think about it this way. A wife knows and could list all the positive qualities and information about her husband. Are all these qualities the LOVE she feels toward him? I don't think so, and I bet neither does she. If I found another man, who has even better qualities than her husband, would she still love him? The answer is that the love she has for her husband is not the sum total of his positive qualities, rather her experience of his love and affection for her.

TRUST then is an action verb and a choice made with your **WILL**. It is not information, thoughts or feelings in your mind. It is that choice to trust, let go, and be vulnerable to open the door to our hearts and soul, to experience and feel another's presence (their consciousness, mind, and soul). By just having faith and believing in Jesus, we operate only with our thoughts, feelings and minds and express our love for the Lord by reciting prayers, devotions and rituals.

Peace, Joy, Life, Forgiveness, Healing, Hope, Strength, and love come through **Trusting in Jesus.**

Now, if the goal of school and God is Trust while we are here in these bodies, then how do we **do it**?

PARABLE OF THE HIGH WIRE WALKER

There was a high wire walker for which millions of people would come from all over the world, just to get a glimpse of him perform incredible and impossible things on the wire without a net, 100 feet in the air.

For one hour he did things that were spell bounding and just down right impossible.

At the end of the hour, there was a grand silence, and the spectators were in awe from what they had seen.

He came down from the wire, approached somebody in the bleachers, and said to them, "What do you think?"

The person responded, "I think that I have never seen anything like what I just witnessed."

The high wire walker then looked the person in the eye and asked, "Who do you say that I am?" The person paused and then said, "From what I've seen, I think that you are the greatest high wire walker that has and will ever live."

"Good," said the high wire walker and looked at the person in the eye again. "Do you believe in me?" The person said, "Yes, I do believe in you."

Then the high wire walker said, "Do you see this wheelbarrow here? It has a smooth solid glass wheel in the front. There are no treads or grooves on it. I am going to bring it up 100 ft. and walk it across the wire, but I am going to chain my hands to the handles, so if the wheelbarrow slips off the wire, and it falls a 100 ft to the ground, I will fall with it."

With great love for the person, the high wire walker looked deep into the person's eyes and said, "Do you believe I can do that?"

The person responded with confidence: "YES, I do believe you can do that!"

*Then with the utmost gentle kindness, the high wire walker said to the person, "**Good...now get inside the wheelbarrow.**"*

STOP:

Use your minds and imagine that Jesus is right there with you now, because He is. Choose to keep focusing on Him and listen carefully to what He is teaching you about how to trust.

JESUS:

Peace be with you. It is Jesus, your friend. Yes, it's me, right here with you.

I want you to choose right now to open your heart and mind to receive all that I have for you. I want you to learn to trust that I am with you every moment, whether you feel and sense my presence, or not.

When I said: *"While you are in the world you will suffer, but don't be afraid, for I overcame the fear of Suffering and Death, and I will be with you every day in your suffering,"* - I meant it. This is the truth, while you are in your earthly body.

By now, you know that life brings you problems and suffering, and you try to think your way through them. When you dwell and worry about them, your mind is so out of control with more and more thoughts and emotions, keeping you from being aware that I am with you. This is what Evil does to you, leaves you alone with just your problems and fear.

So stop doing this to yourself! Do not multiply your suffering this way! Instead, choose to become aware of me like you are now, and rest for a moment with me, in peace.

(Pause your reading, close your eyes, and enjoy imagining the Lord is with you, because He is.)

Now back to class, *and continue to pay attention to everything I want you to learn, experience, and do. Remember, I love you and I want to teach you how to overcome your fears and problems, by walking through them with Me. Amen.*

Like Jesus said: if we do not trust *(get inside the wheelbarrow),* we are left alone with our problems, suffering, fear, worry, doubt and despair *(on the bleachers).* This is why many people become angry with God, leave church, and even lose faith. They believe in God and Jesus, but only if He answers all their prayers and fixes their problems, because if God really loves them, He should heal them and make their problems go away right away. This kind of thinking is Evil's way of keeping believers from having a trusting relationship with Jesus. *(Getting in the wheel barrow)* If we do have a personal relationship with Jesus, Evil will have less and less influence and power over us. Why?...because we are inside the wheelbarrow with

Jesus, conquering fear together.

My guess is that St. Paul and the early Christians who were persecuted and executed because of their faith experienced the power and love of Christ that was greater than their fear of Suffering and Death. They trusted and got inside the wheelbarrow.

> ☐ *"The power in us now is greater than the powers that are in the world." (1 Jn. 4:4)*
> ☐ *"The sufferings of the present are as nothing compared to the glory that God will manifest in us." (Rom. 8:18)*

HERE ARE THE STEPS TO TRUST
WHAT TO DO

No matter what thoughts are in your mind, and no matter how intense your feelings and emotions are:

1. Choose *(with Your **WILL**)* to focus off of the problem, fear, or whatever is tempting you.

2. Focus on Jesus with you by simply saying, "Lord."

3. Keep choosing to stay focused on and say NO to your thoughts, feelings and emotions.

4. Rest in His presence, whether you experience Him or not until you find Peace of Mind.

5. Lastly, replace your negative thoughts, half-truths, and lies that are in your mind causing your fears, worries, and stress—with the Truth and presence of the Lord.

6. Then do His will no matter what you think or feel, constantly aware that He is with you, giving you strength and power to overcome anything.

You really need to imprint the above steps into your mind, memorize it, and from now on call it to mind throughout your day. When you have problems and suffer, build a **TRUST** relationship with the Lord. The heart of this book is that Jesus is teaching you, how to experience Him as the Truth, the Life, and the Way, to answer your questions, what to do about them, and how to do it.

WHAT YOU AND I FORGOT WHEN WE GREW UP: TRUST

I want you to use your memory and imagination.

- ☐ Remember when you were four and not yet in school. See yourself.
- ☐ Remember how you clung to your mother's leg.
- ☐ Remember when your mother told you that you could play outside, but stay in the yard. See yourself playing in the yard.
- ☐ **OUCH!** Remember falling and cutting your knee on the sidewalk and seeing it bleed? You were frightened and screamed, and it sure did hurt. Can you see it?
- ☐ What was the first word out of your mouth? That's right: **Mommy!**
- ☐ You had only one thing in your Mind, and it was not a thing, it was **Mommy.** Then you ran as fast as you could to Mommy. See yourself doing that.
- ☐ The minute Mommy saw you crying and bleeding, she picked you up and held you. Your arms were already certainly open for her embrace.
- ☐ Then your mother held you until you finally calmed down and stopped crying.
- ☐ Now, what did you feel from your Mommy that made you stop crying? _____.
- ☐ Be specific now and list what you experienced and felt when your mother embraced you. _____.
- ☐ My guess is that you felt, comfort, safety, and love.

QUESTIONS FOR YOU:

- ☐ *Were you still afraid?* Perhaps not so much after your mother's love.

- ☐ *Was your knee still bleeding?* Yes.

- ☐ *Did your knee still hurt?* Yes.

Well, what do you know? Let's get this straight: your knee was still bleeding and hurting, but you were OK. You were OK, because you did not just believe in your mother's love, but trusted her *(got inside the wheelbarrow)* and experienced it, by focusing immediately off of the problem and instead on Mommy.

Where was the love, comfort, and safety you felt? It was in your mother, because it <u>was</u> your mother, and when she embraced and held you, it passed from her into you, and delivered you from your fear.

Did your problem (boo-boo) go away immediately? No, but you, were OK.

<u>CONCLUSION</u>: At four years old, you automatically and instinctively followed all the steps to **TRUST** perfectly. Gee, if Life is School, as we have learned, then at four years old you were a senior in high school, because you trusted almost perfectly. Hmm, that is interesting, isn't it?

Everything we **needed** to learn in this life, we knew when we were four: <u>Trust</u>

What happened to you and me that has put us back into Kindergarten, worried and frightened about all of our problems, suffering, and boo-boos in life? We grew up—that is what happened—and because we did, we lost and forgot how to **Trust**, especially in the Lord.

We became our own God, and little by little no longer reached out for the Lord's wisdom, comfort, strength and healing. Why do we need to focus immediately on Jesus first when we cut our knee or have a problem? We can just call 911, a doctor, or get a band-aid. We can get a job, make money, and buy what we want.

"Who needs God? I can do it by myself. I am in control of my life."

In short, we have become more and more independent.

This is very important, because now you are beginning to understand why sometimes it feels like the Lord doesn't care, help, or answer your prayers.

<u>JESUS</u>:

Now you know why I said, **"Unless you become like little children, you will never enter the Kingdom of God."** *Because of Evil, you have been seduced* *into believing that you have total control of your life. It is a false sense of control that distracts and draws your attention away from me and focuses your attention on the pleasure of power and control. The reason it is false is because the physical, mental, and emotional suffering you experience is out of control. This is where all your fear, worrying, discouragement and despair come from. Then, you pray and ask me to fix it so you can find Peace of Mind and rest, and when it does not go away, you blame me for not caring or loving you. This is what Evil wants you to do, not believe or trust Me. At that moment, when you choose not to trust Me, you are alone with your problems and suffering, without hope. This is exactly where Evil has led you, to despair.*

That is what I meant when I said "You must become like little children." You need to retrain your mind, like when you were 4 years old, and do exactly what you said and did back then. Instead of **Mommy,** say **Lord** *and then focus off the problem, pain and suffering, and focus on Me with your whole mind and no other thought or desire except to experience my embrace. Then you will find your answer and what's more—I, your Lord, loves you, like your mother.*

So, remember this truth. I did not come into the world to fix everybody, everything, and all of your problems.

I came into the world to conquer your fear of them, give you rest, and then overcome them together with the power that I overcame mine with.

So keep paying attention and burning the way to trust into your mind, until it replaces the way Evil and the world has taught you. Most of all, remember, I love you and believe in you. Amen!

JESUS NEVER SAID THIS:

    □ *"Come to me all you who labor and are heavy burdened, and I will* ***FIX EVERYTHING."***

JESUS SAID:

    □ *"Come to me all you who labor and are heavy burdened, and I will give you* ***REST****." (Mt. 11:28)*

Just like what our mothers did. Jesus is waiting 24/7 to calm us down, give us rest, Peace of Mind, and deliver us from our fear.

This sure puts life and suffering into a new perspective and on the path to overcoming our problems, **but instead, together with the Lord.**

In the next chapter on Suffering, we will learn **WHAT to do and HOW to** experience the Lord's strength and love with us, every day.

CHAPTER 5:
EVIL HAS INFECTED US WITH SUFFERING AND DEATH. HOW?

Let's be clear. Suffering has the most questions that need answers, not only for you and me but for all humanity as Jesus will teach us later. Suffering and Death are at the core of our existence and lives, and even more at the heart and center of our faith.

Before the Lord answers your questions about Suffering and Death, I want to put some flesh and blood on the word "suffering" so you will get the scope and depth of it and feel it's overwhelming power and horrifying effects on your thoughts, feelings, and emotions.

Cancer; heart failure; Alzheimer's disease; mental illness; mutations; chronic pain; chronic nausea; severe arthritis; spine injury; eating disorders; lung disease; stomach and bowel pain and disorders; chronic migraine headaches; innocent babies, infants, children, suffering and dying in the arms of their parents; somebody's daughter abducted, raped, dismembered, and thrown away like trash.

Terrorism; beheading; torture; genocide; drug addiction; human trafficking; capturing young kids, girls, and women to rape, sell, enslave, and then butcher and kill; school shootings; wars; gassing; bombing; biochemical warfare; mutilation; suffocation; water boarding; abortion; partial birth abortion.

What did they do to deserve it?

Sadly enough, it probably did not take long for you to start reading the above list and experiencing the Evil power that Suffering and Fear has over us. I don't know about you, but I have a hard time digesting and wrapping my head around the whole thing. When it comes to the darkness, depth, and despair, they can be overwhelming and even terrifying.

I created this list to introduce the next and greatest task to understand. And that is suffering.

- Where did it come from?
- Why do we have to suffer?
- Why do little babies have to suffer and die? They are innocent and did nothing wrong.
- Why does God allow it?
- Why do we suffer and have to die?
- If God really loves us, why doesn't He do something about it?

- ☐ If Jesus came to save us from all this Sin, Suffering and Death, where is it, and where is He when we pray?
- ☐ The bottom line is this. If there is no difference or change in Sin, Suffering and Death since Jesus came, why should anyone believe in him as a loving God? What is the use, really?

Many times, these lingering questions are the reasons for believers leaving the church, faith, and religion all together. Without answers, part of me does not blame them. Many Christians who do believe give the answer: You have to have faith.

Somehow this just doesn't cut it when you look into the eyes of parents holding their two-day-old first born child who has less than 24 hours to live. What that answer does is tell the parents that they do not have enough faith for God to heal their child. A consoling answer? I don't think so. Now they are not only in despair, without hope for their baby, but are guilty for not having enough faith, so much for Faith being the answer!

We need answers, and we need them from God. But we need more than just answers. We need God to tell us the truth about suffering. We need God to tell us what to do about suffering, and we need Him to show us how to do it. Without answers, we are disappointed in God and become angry with Him, believing He is a deaf, impotent, and a powerless God lacking love or compassion. This leads to doubt and then despair when we stop praying or talking to the Lord. Then we are left without any hope.

EVIL AND SUFFERING: FINALLY, THE ANSWERS

HOW DID SUFFERING AND DEATH ENTER THE WORLD, AFFECTING ALL OF US & ALL PHYSICAL REALITY?

God does not cause Suffering and Death. **EVIL** does. How did Evil come into the world and all physical reality?

Every major religion, society, and culture has discussed, debating the answer to this question. They've even written it sacred texts. I find that the most detailed and credible texts regarding Evil's origin are from the book of Enoch.

The book of Enoch, found in Qumran in 1948 near the Dead Sea, though not in the Canonical inspired books of the Bible, is one of the oldest of the Creation narratives. The book of Genesis in the Judeo-Christian Bible borrows much from the earlier written Book of Enoch. For our purposes, here is an English translation of the passage describing how Evil came into the world.

BOOK OF ENOCH: *(A brief overview)*

In the Book of Enoch, the "Watchers" are angels dispatched to Earth to watch over the humans. They soon begin to lust for human women and at the prodding of their leader Samyaza (Leader of Fallen Angels), they defect "en masse" to illicitly instruct humanity and procreate with them. The offspring of these unions are the Nephilim, savage giants who pillage the earth and endanger humanity.

Samyaza and his associates further taught their human charges arts and technologies such as weaponry, cosmetics, mirrors, sorcery, and other techniques that would otherwise be discovered gradually over time by humans, not foisted upon them all at once. Eventually God allows a Great Flood to rid the earth of the Nephilim but first sends the Archangel Uriel to warn Noah so as not to eradicate the human race. The Watchers are bound "in the valleys of the Earth" until Judgment Day.

> ☐ *And when their sons have slain one another, and they have seen the destruction of their beloved ones, bind them fast for seventy generations in the valleys of the earth, until the day of their Judgment. In those days, they shall be lead away to the abyss of fire, and to the torment and the prison, in which they shall be confined forever. Whosoever shall be condemned and destroyed will from thenceforth be bound together with them to the end of all generations and destroy all the spirits of the reprobate and the children of the Watchers, because they have wronged mankind. Destroy all wrong from the face of the earth, and let every evil work come to an end: and let the plant of righteousness and truth appear, and it shall prove a blessing; the works of righteousness and truth shall be planted in truth and joy for evermore.*
> ☐ *Enoch, thou scribe of righteousness, go and declare to the Watchers of the Heaven, who have left the high Heaven, the holy eternal place. They have defiled themselves with women, have done as the children of earth do, and have taken unto themselves wives, "Ye have wrought*

great destruction on the earth, and ye shall have no peace, nor forgiveness of sin, and as they delight themselves in their children, the murder of their beloved ones shall they see. And over the destruction of their children shall they lament and shall make supplication unto eternity, but mercy and peace shall ye not attain." (Book of Enoch chapters 6,7,8)

Enoch describes the chronology of Satan and the fallen angels. It illustrates what they chose and what they did to their estate in Heaven, their relationship with God, and to us.

The following are Scriptures that describe the essence of God, who is mystery, yet revealed with His own words. What is important is that all reality in the Spirit World as well as the physical, including you and me, shares in the unconditional love of God. That is, God (described as Light, not light as we know it, but Divinity).

By reflecting on God as Light, we can appreciate who and what we are to God and understand the magnitude of what Satan and the fallen angels lost and can never get back. It is interesting that one of the names associated with Satan and Evil is Lucifer, which means Light.

Put simply, in choosing to be "God" and have his own kingdom, power, and servants (humanity), which he and his fallen angels would corrupt, control, and manipulate with knowledge of Good and Evil, they **lost their Light and the Unconditional Love of God.**

As you read the following Scripture, it will become clear that **God** is **Light**, and all His creation shares and is one with God, without losing their unique identity.

We are beings of Light, but because of what Evil has done to us, there is now darkness, Sin, Suffering and Death.

LIGHT AND DARKNESS
WE ARE LIGHT MADE PHYSICAL

1. "GOD IS LIGHT; in him there is no darkness at all." Note we are not told that God is a light, but that HE IS LIGHT. Light is His essence, as is Unconditional Love.
   (1 Jn. 5)

2. Jesus told them, "You are going to have the light just a little while longer. Walk while you have the light before darkness

overtakes you. Whoever walks in the dark does not know where they are going." *(Jn. 12:35)*

4. "Believe in the light while you have the light, so that you may become children of light." *(Jn. 12:36)*

5. "This is the message we have heard from him and declare to you, God is light; in Him, there is no darkness at all." *(1 Jn. 1:5)*

6. When Jesus spoke again to the people, He said, "I am the light of the world. Whoever follows me will never walk in darkness, but will have the light of life."
   (Jn. 8:12)

7. "Jesus transfigured before them; and his face did shine as the sun, and his garments became white as the light." *(Mt. 17)*

8. "If we do not have the light, we do not know God. Those who know God, who walk with Him, are of the light and walk in the light. They are partakers of God's divine nature, having escaped the corruption in the world caused by evil desires."
   (2 Peter 1:4)

9. "God is light, and so is His Son." Jesus said: I am the light of the world. You are all children of the light and children of the day. We do not belong to the night or to the darkness.
   (1 Thessalonians 5:5)

10. "Light is uncomfortable to those accustomed to the dark."
    (Jn. 3:20)

11. "Jesus, the sinless Son of God, is the true light." *(Jn 1:9)*

12. As adopted sons of God, we are to reflect His light into a world darkened by sin. Our goal in witnessing to the unsaved is "to open their eyes and turn them from darkness to light and from the power of Satan to God." *(Acts 26:18)*

13. "Jesus, the sinless Son of God, is the true light." *(Jn 1:9)*

14. As adopted sons of God, we are to reflect His light into a world darkened by sin. Our goal in witnessing to the unsaved is "to open their eyes and turn them from darkness to light and from the power of Satan to God." *(Acts 26:18)*

To help clarify what all this means in the big picture for you and me, run this through your Mind.

It is the choice between our physical reality subject to our human desires (Sin, Suffering, Death) and God's light. Our physical can never be completely satisfied or removed from temptation or separation from loved ones. I cannot say it any better than God did.

I place before you "Life and Death." Choose Life! (Deut. 30:19)

SUMMARY:

- [ ] God did not create Evil.
- [ ] Conscious spiritual beings, created by God in Heaven were sent to guide and live among humanity—angels.
- [ ] They lusted after human women, seduced and had sex with them, which was forbidden by God, both for humans and the fallen angels.
- [ ] These spiritual beings in physical bodies wanted to be "gods," having their own Kingdom and followers. Because they had knowledge greater than ours, they interfered with our DNA through sex and genetic engineering; cloning; cross breeding; producing evil monsters who taught knowledge to humans that God forbade to give to us.
- [ ] *"We were created a little less than the angels..." (Hebrews 2:7)*
- [ ] Thus, Evil came into the physical realm permanently, and with it, Suffering and Death.

If this sounds like a Science fiction movie and fantasy story (Myth), it may not be anymore, because of recent archeological and scientific discoveries.

- [ ] We now can manipulate chromosomes and DNA.
- [ ] We now can mix different DNAs to create new species.
- [ ] We now are on the cutting edge of artificial intelligence.
- [ ] We now can clone a human body.
- [ ] We are developing mind control techniques

Maybe what the Theologians and Scripture scholars thought was a myth, little by little, became actual recorded history. Remember, I am only speculating here, because of recent discoveries that strongly suggest the possibility.

I find the Book of Enoch the most credible description of the origin of Evil that describes not just as myths and stories but actual recorded historical events. This should wake up theologians and Scripture scholars who are reading this and are loaded to dispute The Book of Enoch as a historical narrative.

My purpose in writing this book is not to give a definitive answer to the Origin of Evil, rather that they are Conscious beings with knowledge and power and realities that exist, affect, and influence us.

WHAT JESUS SAID ABOUT SATAN AND EVIL

"The Enemy"	*Mt. 13:39*
"The Evil One"	*Mt. 13:38*
"The Prince of this world"	*Jn. 12:31*
"A Liar" & "The father of lies"	*Jn. 8:44*
"A murderer"	*Jn. 8:44*
"The tempter"	*Mt. 4:3*
"The Prince of demons"	*Mt. 12:24*
"He perverts the Scripture"	*Mt. 4:4*
"The god of this world"	*II Cor. 4:4*
"The deceiver" of the whole world"	*Rev. 12:9*
"The great dragon; the old serpent"	*Rev. 12:9*
"The seducer of Adam and Eve"	*Gen. 3:1-20*
"He has a Kingdom"	*Mt. 12:26*
"Evil men are his sons"	*Mt. 13:38*
"eternal fire is prepared for him"	*Mt. 25*
"Seeks to devour Christians"	*1 Peter 5*

CONCLUSION:

- ☐ Does the devil and Evil really exist? The language of Jesus certainly indicates his own belief in the existence of a personal devil.
- ☐ Satan and Evil have affected, rather infected, all of physical reality, which includes our physical bodies—brain included. In turn, Evil can infest our **MINDS** with thoughts and images that awaken our emotions, feelings, desires, passions, and affect our choices, if we let it.

☐ Evil, ultimately intends to seduce, control, enslave, destroy us, and use us to destroy each other.

Take of moment to read the above three conclusions and remember them. Why? You cannot defeat the Enemy, unless you know who they are, and how they operate.

According to Jesus and the New Testament, Satan and Evil exist. Conscious beings with divine knowledge have powers. If you do not believe in this, remember your problem is not with me, but with Jesus.

☐ *"The one who does what is sinful is of the devil, because the devil has been sinning from the beginning. The reason the Son of God appeared was to destroy the devil's work." (1 Jn. 3:8)*
☐ *"I am afraid that just as Eve was deceived by the serpent's cunning, **your minds** may somehow be led astray from your sincere and pure devotion to Christ." (2 Corinthians 11:3)*
☐ *"Submit yourselves then to God. Resist the devil, and he will flee from you." (James 4:7)*

If all this Satan and Evil talk is starting to frighten you, relax, because there is not only good but **Great News** coming. By the time you finish this book, Satan and Evil will be frightened and terrified of **YOU**.

EVIL EXPOSED: HOW IT AFFECTS OUR MINDS

To recapitulate, we know that Evil exists and its intention when it comes to all physical reality. That is, it is to ultimately destroy God's creation and humanity, you and me included. Now we can unmask its powers, how it operates and affects our minds and bodies.

If you need to, page back to the **Chapter: Who and What We Are**, and read again about what your Mind is. It is **not** physical, flesh and blood.

> **THIS IS WHAT THE LORD WANTS TO GIVE YOU AUTHORITY AND POWER OVER.**
>
> *These are the signs that will follow all those who believe... They will cast out evil spirits and demons.*
>
> - The only thing evil spirits and demons (conscious non-physical beings) can do is put THOUGHTS and IMAGES into your Mind.
> - Evil cannot touch your WILL, unless we let it by choosing to think about the thoughts and images placed in our Minds and dwell on them.
> - Because our altered DNA has infected our physical brains, minds, and bodies, we choose to think about and dwell on thoughts and images that ignite our fears, desires, and passions.

If the only thing Evil can do is put thoughts and images in your minds, then your Mind is the battlefield where you are in continual warfare with Evil that is trying to seduce, control your Will and decisions, and ultimately destroy you and all of us.

SCRIPTURE: REGARDING YOUR MIND

Romans 12:2

> *Do not be conformed to this world but be transformed by the renewal of your mind, that by testing **(Life is school)** you may discern what is the will of God, what is good and acceptable and perfect.*

1 Corinthians 2:13-16

> *We impart this in words not taught by human wisdom, but taught by the Spirit, interpreting spiritual truths to those who are spiritual. The natural person does not accept the things of the Spirit of God, for they are folly to him, and he is not able to understand them, because they are spiritually discerned. The spiritual person judges all things but himself to be judged by no one. For who has understood the mind of the Lord so as to instruct him. **But we have the mind of Christ**.*

2 Timothy 1:7

☐ *For God gave us a spirit not of fear, but of power and love and self-control.*

Jesus is teaching us that, in fact, we are in school, and He is retraining our Minds to think and operate the way His does. This is not a "one time deal," but takes a whole lifetime to learn and get better at it. The good news is the more we do it, the better we get, and the more natural it becomes.

On a personal note, one of the main goals for me is to experience and be able to say before I graduate from school what St. Paul said, *It is no longer I who live, but Christ Jesus my Lord that lives in me. (Gal. 2:29)* The point here is that the Lord is telling you what to do and how to do it every day. The more you replace the negative thoughts, images, half-truths, and lies that Evil and the world infest your mind with every day, the more you will feel the freedom from your fear and worrying.

☐ *"Finally, brothers, whatever is true, whatever is honorable, whatever is just, whatever is pure, whatever is lovely, whatever is commendable, if there is any excellence, if there is anything worthy of praise, think about these things." (Phil. 4:8)*

HOW EVIL WORKS: PAY CLOSE ATTENTION!

1. Evil puts thoughts and images in your mind, tempting you to choose, download, and think about them.

2. When you choose to think about them, that is when powers and spirits can almost immediately enter your feelings, emotions and desires, with fear, anxiety, lust, anger, etc.

3. When you continue to **DWELL** on them, they intensify your emotions and desires to act on them. This can lead to obsession, when you cannot stop your mind from thinking about and dwelling on your problems or suffering. This is like putting gasoline on the fire of your passions and desires.

4. Then you become like a volcano ready to erupt and the only way to release these desires and emotions is to act on them and do the Evil that promises you pleasure and satisfaction.

5. When you succumb to this temptation and attack, you choose (Your WILL) to do the Evil.

It's like a computer. I hope you are a little computer savvy. If you are, then you have probably seen the irritating blue screen with the message that your computer is infected with a virus. Doesn't it frustrate you? And it usually happens when you are right in the middle of something important.

Next is that little icon at the bottom of the screen that starts pulsating. And the following message pops up: "Your computer is infected with a Virus. Click here and download a free program that will clean your hard drive from the virus."

Here is the question for you: Should you click on the free anti-virus program that promises to restore your computer? If you are computer literate, your answer is NO. **Why, because it is the VIRUS.**

This is exactly how Evil works on our Minds. It promises you everything, but in the end destroys you and others. Evil has power over us while we are in these physical bodies, because they have not only interfered with our DNA physically but also our Minds and infected them with the capacity to "know" and experience Good and EVIL.

This is one of the reasons Jesus came to save us, that is, to give us the authority and power over Evil. The only problem is that many clergy and religious leaders never taught us about Jesus power to deliver and how to use it. The good news here is that Jesus will teach you how, later in this book. Be patient, He will do this later and do it with you. Now that is something to get excited about and look forward to!

St. Paul describes the battle that goes on in our minds and how Evil has power over us.

> I know that the law is spiritual; but I am unspiritual, sold as a slave to sin. I do not understand what I do. For what I want to do I do not do, but what I hate I do. If I do what I do not want to do, I agree that the law is good. As it is, it is no longer I, myself, who do it, but it is sin living in me. For I know that good itself does not dwell in me, that is, in my sinful nature. I have the desire to do what is good, but I cannot carry it out. For I do not do the good I want to do, but the Evil I do not want to do—this I keep on doing. Now if I do what I do not want to do, it is no longer I who do it, but it is sin living in me that does it.

- *Therefore, I find this law at work, although I want to do Good, Evil is right there with me. For in my inner being I delight in God's law; but I see another law at work in me, waging war against the law of my mind and making me a prisoner of the law of sin at work within me. What a wretched man I am! Who will rescue me from this body, that is subject to death? Thanks be to God, who delivers me, through Jesus Christ our Lord! (Romans 8:1)*
- *So then, I myself in my mind am a slave to God's law, but in my sinful nature a slave to the law of sin. (Romans 7)*

Let us take this and apply how Evil works on our minds, with an issue of the day. The following is an article I wrote and submitted to a local newspaper.

EXAMPLE: <u>IDENTITY POLITICS</u>

My greatest fear is that Identity Politics has led us to divisions, not only in our political views, but in our churches, communities, and what's worse: in our families and with our friends. From division, Identity Politics has led to anger and then to violent anger that wants to retaliate and punish. The more we engage in it, the more we become obsessed by it, demonize people, and are filled with hatred. The final choice is open harassment, violence, and then civil war.

I believe the power and forces that are driving this are not just part of our human nature, but demonic. Evil is the one word that is mentioned often, but never discussed, understood, or addressed how it <u>seduces</u>, <u>influences</u>, <u>and then controls</u> people's minds, will, and actions. Maybe it is time to not only discuss answers and solutions to the issues, but also the evil forces that are the real enemy influencing, obsessing and possessing terrorists, rapists, murderers, traffickers, gangs, and even ourselves.

*In the Christian Scripture it says, **"Our struggle is not against flesh and blood, but against the rulers, principalities and powers of this dark world and the spiritual forces of Evil in the heavenly realms."** (Eph. 6:12) The reason Evil seems to be triumphing is that most people do not believe in Satan or Evil powers. Not a bad tactic on Satan's part to keep people powerless by their choice to not believe, while He's busy achieving his ends without any resistance.*

*Politicians, media, news networks and their "so called" professional panels, debates and "reliable" sources have produced NO answers or solutions but only division and have given birth to their evil child: **Identity Politics**. Identity Politics is merely the "politically correct" term for hate and demonizing those* who disagree with us. The hidden and inherent evil in identity politics is the "Self Righteous Justification" Evil uses to, little by little, control our minds with negative thoughts, half-truths and lies that overwhelm and drive us to violence.

Evil is the real enemy, but for the most part no one wants to talk about it, and those that do are considered out of touch with reality. Yet, Satan and Evil, or what ever you call them has existed and has been experienced from the beginning of humanity and recorded in every major and ancient religion. Evil does not need our belief in it to exist. It does exist and my guess is that most of us have heard, seen, or experienced something that seemed so surreal that our minds were unable to comprehend it. And we recoiled in terror because it was beyond human. Because we do not acknowledge its existence, we give it free reign to influence our minds, will, and actions.

*Personally, I am tired of Politics, Media, News Networks, Panels, Experts, Republicans and Democrats. I'm tired of narratives, and most of all I'm tired of words, words, and more words that **Identity Politics** offers—words that fuel demonizing people, hatred, and violence. This is my attempt to expose the real enemy, Evil, and what it has done and is doing to people and humanity. My prayer is that this will be a "wake up" call for all of us tempted and seduced by Identity Politics. Let's cross the divide, close ranks and focus **only** on finding real answers and solutions for real people. My hope is to begin the conversation to understand and call out Evil and develop a strategy to combat and cast it out of our conversations.*

This article demonstrates how Evil, by our choosing to download, think about, and dwell on the thoughts and images it puts in our minds, progresses to a point where we are driven to act on them— ultimately destroying ourselves and maybe others.

I categorize these Evil thoughts into:

- ☐ **NEGATIVE THOUGHTS**: Doctor: "I'm sorry, but your tests came back positive."
- ☐ **HALF-TRUTHS**: "You are terminal and going to die."
- ☐ **LIES**: "Death is the end of your existence and life."

ANSWER: HOW TO "CAST OUT" EVIL THOUGHTS FROM YOUR MIND

Using the analogy of NOT clicking on and downloading the free program to delete the virus in your computer, because it <u>is</u> the **Virus**, don't download the evil thoughts or images.

HERE ARE THE STEPS:

1. **Say NO** the minute you become aware that you are afraid, or being tempted and seduced. Use your <u>WILL</u> and choose to say **NO**.

15. **Then Say, LORD,** the same as you did the minute you experienced a problem or suffering when you were four and cried out for Mommy. This step is not magic, but the most difficult of all, and the essential element to getting your degree in Trust. You are using your **WILL** to say **NO** and choosing to focus off the negative thoughts, half-truths and lies and on Jesus right there with you. Evil is not going to give up attacking and tempting you, especially when it has successfully trained your mind for years to download everything into your mind and immediately think about and dwell on them. In this step, you will need to say <u>**NO**</u> many times, and probably for the rest of your earthly life, because this is the way the Lord will retrain your Mind.

EXAMPLE: The doctor tells you the results of your tests: they are positive for cancer. This is a serious negative thought, right? If you choose to download and think about it, immediately a flood of more half-truths and lies enter like, "Its terminal; I know it, I'm going to die. It's the end of my life; What about my family?"

Then the images of suffering download and "How am I going to deal with this? I can't do it." Does this sound familiar? And the worst is yet to come—Fear. The more you choose to think and dwell on those incoming thoughts and images, the more intense they get. Your emotions and feelings kick in almost instantly, and Fear turns into terror, as you see there is no way out. Your mind keeps racing and racing out of control. It is at this point that people of faith pray and ask God to help them to make the problem go away, be healed and put to rest. If they keep praying and praying, and the cancer or problem does not go away, gets worse, and death is immanent—the next lie of Evil is "You're wasting your time praying and going to church. If God really loved you like He said, He would heal you."

This is "the moment of truth" for you and your relationship with Jesus. Are you going to Trust Him no matter what, or are you going to succumb to the Fear and Evil's lies that are tempting you to

Doubt. If you choose to Doubt and stop trusting in the Lord, Evil will lead you into the dark hole of despair, with only your problem and without hope. This is, as I said before, the goal of Evil—to destroy you and keep you from the power of the Lord and the Truth.

Focusing on the Lord with you is an act of Trust, which is what we are here in school to learn and grow in.

<u>JESUS</u>:

*Remember when I said that the TRUTH will set you free? I meant it. More importantly, I said that I myself am the Truth, the Way and the Life. The Truth you seek is not just a thought, but an experience of my love for you, so read and memorize the Truth about Anger, Suffering, Guilt, and Death. Then memorize Evil's lies, and from now on say **NO** to them, reject them, do not let them in. Instead, focus on the Truth and me until you are able to set yourself free from fear. Stay with me, like you did when you ran to your mother. Keep reading, because there is more good news to come.*

1. **REPLACE** the negative thoughts, half-truths, and lies with the TRUTH.

<u>EXERCISE</u>: Take your time when reading the Truths to replace those evil thoughts that are at the root of much of your suffering. Memorize them, burn the Truth in your mind and use the truth to counteract the evil thoughts.

<u>FEAR/ANGER/DOUBT/DESPAIR</u>

LIES-HALF-TRUTHS- NEGATIVE THOUGHTS:

- ☐ Death is the End.
- ☐ The tests will be positive— I know it. I'll never endure this.
- ☐ Why is God punishing me?
- ☐ What's the use of praying? God isn't doing anything.

<u>TRUTH</u>: **Jesus, what do you say?**

- ☐ *"Don't be afraid or let your hearts be troubled. Trust in God and trust in Me." (Jn. 14:27)*
- ☐ *"I am with you every day until the end of time." (Mt. 28:20)*

- *"Where there is fear, love has not been perfected, love dispels fear." (1 Jn. 4:18)*
- *"While you are in the world you will suffer (and your bodies will die), but don't be afraid, for I overcame my fear of Suffering and Death and will be with you in yours." (Jn. 16:33)*

GUILT/SELF-HATRED

LIES-HALF-TRUTHS- NEGATIVE THOUGHTS:

- I hurt others deeply. I am selfish and destroyed someone and myself.
- I can never get back what I lost. God could never forgive me. I am embarrassed, ashamed, and just want to hide. I'm going to hell. This feeling of guilt will never go away, no matter what I do. I don't like myself for what I did. I don't think I can live with this every day, for the rest of my life.

TRUTH:

- To the woman caught in adultery, Jesus said: "Does anyone condemn you, then **neither do I condemn you.** Go and sin no more." *(Jn. 8)*
- *What I do, I do not understand, for I do not do what I want, but what I hate. For I do not do the good I want, but I do the Evil I do not want. Because I am a slave to sin, what a wretched man I am! Who will deliver me from this mortal body? "Praise be my Lord Jesus Christ for those who are in Him, there is NO condemnation!" (Romans 8)*
- The Prodigal Father never asked his son who returned home what he did or what his sins were. He said, "Put rings on his fingers, give him a cloak, kill the fatted calf, and let's celebrate. *(Lk. 15)*
- The Lord unconditionally loves you before you sin, while you are sinning, and after. His love for you never changes. *Look at a Crucifix and you'll see it.*

SUFFERING

LIES-HALF-TRUTHS- NEGATIVE THOUGHTS:

- I will never be able to go through it.
- It will always hurt this badly and get even worse.
- Where is God, and why me?

- I can't take it anymore.
- I won't be able to do the things I use to. What's the use of living?
- It is so frustrating. Will it ever stop?
- I don't understand why we have to suffer for so long. Life is hell.

TRUTH:

- *"Therefore, we are not discouraged; rather, although our outer self (physical body) is wasting away, our inner self is being renewed day by day." (2 Cor. 4:16)*
- *"For this momentary suffering is producing for us an eternal glory beyond all comparison, as we look not to what is seen but to what is unseen; for what is seen is transitory, but what is unseen is eternal." (2 Cor. 4:18)*
- *"The sufferings of the present are as nothing, compared to the Glory that will be revealed in us." (Rom. 8:18-23)*
- *"While you are in the World you will suffer, but don't be afraid, for I overcame the world....and I am with you every day, until the end of time." (Jn. 16:13)*
- *"If we share and experience the sufferings of Christ, we will share in His resurrection." (Rom. 8:17)*

DEATH

LIES- HALF-TRUTHS- NEGATIVE THOUGHTS:

- I am dying. It is the end of my life, dead, forgotten, wake, funeral, and buried.
- I will never see my loved ones or experience joy and happiness again.
- I can't stop thinking about it, and I'm afraid of the suffering ahead and my life ending.
- This is it. I'm never getting out of this one. What is going to happen to my family and loved ones?
- I am so frightened and feel so alone and abandoned by God.

TRUTH:

- *"Our Citizenship and Home is in Heaven, and from it we also await a Savior, the Lord Jesus Christ." (Phil. 3:20)*
- *"I am the Resurrection and the Life. Any one who believes in me will never die, and any one who dies believing in me will live forever. (Jn. 11:25)*

☐ *We can't even begin to imagine how great will be the Glory that the Lord will manifest in us." (Rom. 8:18)*

☐ *"For if we have been united with him in a death like his, we will certainly be united with him in His resurrection. (Rom. 6:5)*

☐ *"Do not let your hearts be troubled. Have faith in God; have faith in me. In my Father's house, there are many dwelling places. I will come back again and take you to myself, so that where I am, you also may be." (Jn. 14:1)*

CHAPTER 6:
ATTACKING EVIL AND WINNING: WHAT TO DO AND HOW TO DO IT!

Are you scared yet with all this talk about Satan and Evil? Is your Fear thermometer rising with thoughts that there just may be more than the Evil humanity generates? Well, according to what God said about Satan, Evil has and continues to corrupt humanity and all physical reality with the intention to tempt, experiment with, enslave, steal our Light, soul, consciousness, and ultimately destroy us. I offer as proof that this is real by the Fear that enters your mind when you consider and think about Satan and Evil. Why? Fear is Evil's greatest power.

I found the following article that will put some flesh and blood reality on what Satan and Evil are up to, according to the Word of God and what Jesus said about them.

BUSY by Ralph Andrus

Satan called a worldwide convention of demons. In his opening address to his evil angels, he said, "We can't keep Christians from going to church. We cannot keep them from reading their Bibles and knowing the truth. We can't even keep them from holding onto their conservative values, but we can do something else. We can keep them from forming an intimate lasting relationship and experience with Christ. If they gain that connection with Jesus, our power over them is broken.

So, this is what I want you to do. I want you to distract them from experiencing Jesus Christ and having a personal relationship with Him, throughout their day. Let them go to church, let them have their conservative lifestyles, but steal their time so they cannot gain that experience and relationship with Jesus.

The Evil angels asked him, **"How shall we do this?**

- ☐ *Keep them busy with the nonessentials of life to occupy their minds with more things to buy and more things to do.*
- ☐ *Tempt them to spend, spend, then charge, charge, and charge it.*
- ☐ *Convince husbands and wives to work long hours and overtime so they can afford their lifestyles. This will keep them from spending time with their families and talking to Jesus.*
- ☐ *See to it that every store and restaurant in the world plays suggestive and seductive music, trashing Christian values. This will **jam** their minds and break their relationship with Jesus.*

- *Fill their coffee tables with magazines and newspapers. Pound their minds with the news 24 hours a day. Invade their driving moments with billboards. Flood their mailboxes with junk mail, sweepstakes, mail order catalogs and every kind of newsletter and promotion offering free products, services and false hopes.*
- *Even in their recreation, let them be excessive with working out, hunting, fishing, yoga, sports and more sports. Have them return from their recreation exhausted, stressed, and less time for faith and family.*
- *When they go to church, involve them in gossip and small talk, and make them bored so their minds wander off to all the things and activities they have become addicted to. They'll keep checking their watches, wishing the service to hurry up and be over. That way they won't experience Jesus while they are there (Andrus, 2007).*

INTERESTING, ISN'T IT?

Like I said before, Evil wants us to doubt and deny its existence, because by doing so, it renders us powerless over it and gives it free reign to complete its agenda. Somehow, I believe we all know it is real because of our inability to wrap our minds around genocide, mass murders, rape, child abuse, torture, beheading which even the media labels "demonic."

This core belief and response to Evil is in us, because despite being influenced and infected by it, we are still beings of Light, connected to God, which enables us to recognize both Good and Evil—in this case, Evil.

The Word of God describes these beings, entities or powers as the real Enemy.

- *"Our battle is not against flesh and blood, but against Powers, Principalities, and Rulers from the Kingdom of Darkness." (Eph. 6:12)*
- *"When you pray, say, Our Father who art in Heaven...**Deliver Us From Evil.***" (Mt. 6:13)*
- *"These are the signs that will follow all those who believe, whomever they lay their hands on will be healed... In my name, they will cast out demons and spirits." (Mk. 16:17-18)*

STOP:

The above words of God and Jesus are critical for all who read this book and for all of humanity. Read them again one more time before proceeding.

The reason they are critical is that Jesus overcame the temptations of Satan for power, greed, and desire when He was tempted in the desert. When He was condemned, scourged, and crucified, He overcame the temptation of doubt, despair, fear of Suffering, and Death. He did so by choosing to focus on His Father, moment by moment, instead of the temptation and suffering. And He chose with His WILL to Trust the Father. Now do you see the importance, at the beginning of this book, to understand who and what we are as Consciousness, Soul, Mind, and WILL?

Just as Jesus conquered Evil through the power of His Will and Trust, while in a flesh and blood body like ours, now He has paved the way and shown us what to do, how to attack, defeat, and deliver others and ourselves from Evil.

St. Paul said, as noted before,

- *Our battle is not against flesh and blood, but against Powers, Principalities, and Rulers from the Kingdom of Darkness. (Eph. 6:12)*
- *The power that is in us now is greater than the powers that are in the world. (Eph. 1:19)*

I thought at this time it would be helpful to clarify the difference between Deliverance and Possession, which I have found very confusing to people when talking about or experiencing evil spirits or powers. I found the following psychological descriptions of conditions and accompanying manifestations. In addition to defining them, they also offer answers and therapeutic guidelines in dealing with the people who are experiencing this phenomenon. Being in the deliverance ministry, I have found them to be very helpful in developing an appropriate spiritual and psychological approach when ministering with a person for their deliverance.

OPPRESSION – OBSESSION – POSSESSION

PSYCHO-SPIRITUAL TERMS for the conditions, less than Possession, that respond to the commands of authority to dispel forces of Evil are called Oppression and Obsession.

In a state of **OPPRESSION**, people experience attacks of evil spirit from outside of themselves. The most common characteristic of oppression is a sense of heaviness about the head. Frequently people find it difficult to think out a situation or persevere in a task. They feel discouraged and impeded by alien pressures; that is, forces not coming from within themselves. Such persons alone, or in prayer with another, should command in the name of Jesus that the spirit of oppression leave and not return.

In the case of **OBSESSION**, the evil spirits are in a position to create severe disturbances in a particular area within a person. There is an actual presence within the person, though. That presence is NOT in a position to control the person. The person can still exercise free will in determining his or her life. The person can also expel the evil spirits, though often, another person is necessary to assist or direct the deliverance. The person ministering deliverance should have the obsessed person utilize as much spiritual authority as possible. In obsession, the goal is to have the person obsessed arrive at the point of repenting of all past sins and present sinful attitudes, renounce the spirit obsessing them and with the minister, command such spirit or spirits in the name of Jesus to depart and not return.

Put simply, **POSSESSION** is a person who has lost their **Will** completely and the power to choose. The spirit, entity, or demon(s) are in total control of the person, able to manifest their demonic powers. For practical purposes, the Ritual of Exorcism is reserved *(by the local bishop)*, at least in the Catholic Tradition, to an appointed trained "Exorcist." An "Exorcist" is needed, because a possessed person has no Will left that is functioning. This is unlike deliverance where the person prays and works together with others to deliver themselves, as suggested in the case of **OBSESSION**.

*Good News:** If you think you are possessed, you are **NOT**.

BOTH OPPRESSION AND OBSESSION may require physical examination and psychiatric assessment to deal with personal issues for the deliverance and healing to take place. Specific diseases, like Parkinson's disease, can cause certain psychotic manifestations as well as chemical deficiencies. Both have medical therapy treatments.

This is why before praying for deliverance, I ask the person if they have talked to a medical doctor or psychiatrist about their experience. In other words, don't assume that evil spirits are attacking the person or entities no matter what they see or hear. If you do assume that and jump right in praying for deliverance, this may be counter-productive by falsely suggesting and affirming that the person is experiencing the demonic and may even be possessed. **NOT GOOD!**

*CAUTION: With all this talk about Evil and Deliverance, don't start looking for Satan and Evil in everything and everybody. Evil loves your attention and curiosity. Do not give it one iota of your attention. Keep your focus and attention on the Lord with you, and if you feel tempted or finding yourself thinking about it too much, simply tell it to *"Get lost in the name of Jesus"* and forget about it

JESUS:

- ☐ *"The power that is in you now is greater than the powers that are in the world."*
- ☐ *"While you are in the world you will suffer, but don't be afraid of it, or let your hearts be troubled, because I overcame my fear of it, and so will you, because I am with you now."*
- ☐ *"I will never abandon you. You are not alone. I am with you, and always will be. So don't abandon me."*

You will hear these Scriptures repeated often while reading this book, because they are essential for you to not only remember them, but also call them to mind regularly. Try to memorize them and train your brain to use them, to dispel your fears and worries.

*There are Rituals for Deliverance that I use in Chapter 16. You are more than welcome to use them. Remember, don't just go around looking for Evil in everybody and everything. Follow the steps in Chapter 16.

CHAPTER 7:
ANSWERS TO SUFFERING WHAT TO DO & HOW TO DO IT!

If Jesus conquered Evil's temptations and his Fear of Suffering and Death,

- ☐ Why does God allow us to suffer?
- ☐ Why do innocent children have to suffer?
- ☐ Why do some people suffer more than others do?
- ☐ If Jesus loves us, why doesn't He do something about all the horrific Evil in the world?

The following is perhaps the most life changing wisdom that will put you on the path to Peace of Mind, hope, and graduation. I encourage you to read this chapter carefully and slowly, taking moments to stop, reflect, and begin to change what you initially thought about suffering.

What Jesus accomplished and won for us on the cross is liberation from the bondage and slavery to Evil and Fear. In this chapter, Jesus will answer all of your questions and will teach you how to think about suffering, what to do about suffering, and how to do it. What to do and how to do it was never taught to me in the seminary. I had good instructors who explained the Scriptures, theology, and solid intellectual truths, but never what to do. I especially was not guided to experience Jesus' help and healing when in the midst of suffering.

Despite how great my professors were teaching me the faith and the teachings of the Church, what was missing was how to react to my suffering and others, by experiencing Jesus with me. I'm not blaming them, because maybe they didn't know either. And that's why so many books have been written about suffering and the mystery surrounding it. Maybe I was looking out the window in class, which is probably the more credible truth.

Therefore, what Jesus is going to share with you now is what He shared and taught me. My prayer for you as you read this chapter is that you will open your mind and heart to experience the wisdom of the Holy Spirit and the love of your God for you.

ANSWERS FROM JESUS HIMSELF

WHY DO WE SUFFER? "Trust" is the goal, and God does not cause problems, Suffering, and Death.

1. God does not cause Suffering and Death. Evil does. Jesus came to give us the authority and power to dispel and cast Evil out.

2. God allows it and uses it as an opportunity for us to grow in TRUST and overcome fear, worry, and doubt. We have the freedom to make the choices. Will we submit to temptation, fear, doubt, and despair **or** choose the truth, experience the Unconditional Love of God in preparation for eternal life in Heaven, when we leave our physical bodies? *(ref. **Chapter 1**: YOU, your Consciousness, Mind, Will & Soul)*

Remember, you are in School. The way to develop your WILL to trust when you experience problems or devastating suffering is to choose to focus on the Lord instead. If you do not, you will be seduced and sucked into temptation and fear by focusing on the problem, temptation, suffering, and being distracted. This can be interpreted as Looking out the window in school and not paying attention to the Teacher (Jesus) right there with you.

Jesus said and gave you the authority and power over Evil and temptation.

- *"When Jesus had called the Twelve together, he gave them power and authority to drive out all demons and to cure diseases." (Mt. 10:1)*
- *"Jesus told His disciples, "Behold I **give** unto you **power** to tread upon serpents." (Lk. 10:19)*
- *"These signs shall follow them that believe. In my name shall they cast out devils." (Mk. 16:17)*

HOW TO "WIN" & BEAT EVIL

How do you defeat Evil, when FEAR is torturing your Mind with negative thoughts? The key word here is **Win**. When you hear the word **Win**, you are probably thinking about competition or sports. I offer the following analogy to face the enemy and have God fix and make them go away.

COACH ANALOGY

If you are a coach and reading this, I have a question for you. If your team was undefeated during the whole season, and you were in the National Championship game with another team who was undefeated to see who were the better players, would you settle to win the trophy and the National Championship because on the day of the game the other undefeated team forfeited?

Hey, you won the trophy and the National Championship, didn't you? Then why not take it? You would probably hand the trophy and title of champions back, because you never faced the enemy and beat them. It possibly would not feel like a true victory.

Now you know one of the reasons why God allows suffering. In the school paradigm, facing your problems and suffering are your quizzes, tests, and exams. Learning how to Trust is your personal choice to pay attention to all your training on how to win, and then do it. In other words, you cannot do 50 pushups until you can do one. When you start doing all the exercises and prayers and rituals in this book on a regular basis, then you have done your first pushup. If you don't keep doing them daily, then you'll never do 50, just like you'll never pass into the first, second, or third grade of TRUST.

Now you know what Jesus meant when *He said, I have given you authority and power over all Evil and to defeat the enemy. (Mk. 16:17)*

Now you know why this is The Most Important Book You'll Ever Read, because now you are finally getting all the answers, what to do, and HOW TO DO IT!

PRAISE YOU, JESUS!

JESUS:

- ☐ Nothing can or will separate you from Me and My love for you, anguish, distress, persecution, famine, nakedness, danger, or the sword. No! In all these you can and will be more than conquerors through my presence **with** you, for the power the Father and I give you is greater than the powers that are in the world.

> *While you are in the world, you will suffer, but don't be afraid of it because I overcame THE FEAR of Suffering and am **with** you every day to over come yours.*

Problems, Suffering, and Death are **not** the enemy, but Fear of them is. Jesus just gave you the answer of what to do and how to do it. Do you get it? What do you think He is teaching you about how to do it?

STOP: Please read the above Scriptures again and then continue.

The key word is "**WITH**". I have a question for you. When you have problems and suffer, do you say a prayer, go to church, light a candle, and that's it? Do you then try to fix your problem by yourself and expect Jesus to make it go away magically, because you prayed? Then when you are still frightened, you have doubts if Jesus cares.

The reason you have doubts is that no one taught you that Jesus is "**WITH**" you or how to experience Him, His love, strength, and overcome your FEARS. Well get ready, get excited, get pumped, because here is the answer, and it is from Jesus Himself.

> *"In all these you can and will be more than conquerors through my presence **with** you, for the power the Father and I give you is greater than the powers that are in the world." (Mk. 16:17)*

If this sounds familiar, that's because I just had you read it. Contained in this Scripture by St. Paul is the **person and presence of Jesus** that will deliver you from your fear and worrying. Again, the key word is **With**. In other words, if you experience Jesus presence with you, while you are in the midst of suffering and problems, His presence will continually deliver you from your fear while you deal with your situation. Your next question is, "Well, how do you do this?"

HERE'S HOW

Let's take what the Lord taught us about TRUST and apply it to suffering, problems, and our fear of them. I want you to recall the analogy of when you were a child, hurt yourself, and immediately called out for Mommy. Remember, she lifted you up, and held you until you stopped crying. When you stopped crying, you were no longer afraid and instead felt loved, safety and peace. Don't you wish sometimes that you could be back there in her arms as an adult? I know I do.

Here is the rest of my story on how my mother healed and delivered me from my fear. After I cut my knee and it bled, I screamed for my mother, ran to her, and she picked me up and held me until I stopped crying and was no longer afraid. She placed me down, and together we went into the bathroom. I sat on the toilet seat, and she opened the medicine cabinet to take out gauze and some robust medication that stung terribly.

As my mother sat on the edge of the bathtub, she lifted my bloody painful knee up and put it on her lap. The minute I looked at it, my lip curled, and I was frightened again, **BUT** this time having ran first to my mother, **TRUSTING** her, and experiencing her love and comfort, I looked at her sitting on the edge of the tub and felt her presence with me again. This self-assured awareness between focusing on my pain and suffering and my mother continued until she finished bandaging my cut.

HERE ARE SOME KEY QUESTIONS.

- ☐ Did my mother fix my boo-boo? No!
- ☐ Did my pain go away? No, **BUT** I was **OK** and not afraid. Then my mother would give me a hug and reassure me that I was **OK** and say, "Why don't you go back outside and play?"

HOW TO EXPERIENCE THE LORD WITH YOU

Immediately say NO to the negative thoughts and images, and focus off the problem and suffering. Choose with your **WILL** to Trust and focus and be aware of Jesus, right there with you, because He is and asked this of you. Keep doing it until you are at peace, even if the pain and problem does not go away immediately, just like my hurt knee.

Then after giving it to the Lord, let go of it. **HOW**, by not thinking about or dwelling on your problem and PLAY. Do something that will grab your attention, and have fun.

I do believe Jesus is teaching you to play and enjoy life the best you can, once He delivers you from your Fear and leads you "through the valley of shadows and death, to green pastures." Now you know how to do it with Him. Remember, it is not magic, but the good news is the more you practice and retrain your brain and mind to do it, the easier and better it becomes.

PERSONAL WITNESS: When Jesus first taught me this and how to do it, I cannot put into words the liberation and freedom I experienced, like a divine light turned on in my head. I was soaring like an eagle. It was not knowledge or understanding but the power of real Wisdom. It felt like a real embrace of the Lord with and in me.

That is what I am praying for you as you continue to read what the Lord has and wants for you when it comes to experiencing your problems, suffering, and fears.

JESUS NEVER SAID:

Come to me all you labor and are heavy burdened and I will **FIX** *it.*

HE SAID:

Come to me all you who labor and are heavy burdened and I will give you **REST**. *(Mt. 11:28)*

I have come to give you Joy and to make your Joy complete. (Jn. 15:11)

Remember, you are in school, and this is one of the greatest lessons to learn and do every day, all day. As I said before, this is not magic, and you may not feel or experience anything. Do not be discouraged, because you might be doing this for the first time. Remember, you can't do 50 pushups until you can do one. Do your homework, and choose to first Trust the Lord whenever you have a problem, and keep doing it. I promise you, you will begin to be more and more aware that He is with you, and you will be less and less afraid.

THANK YOU JESUS.

<u>STOP READING</u>:

Take a moment and think of a few things to thank the Lord for from just today, and thank Him.

Jesus, I want to thank you for...

WHY GOD SEEMS TO NOT ANSWER YOUR PRAYERS

1. If God really loves me, then why does He seem like an absentee landlord when I pray?

2. Sometimes I think God isn't listening or even cares about what I am going through.

3. Why do I pray and pray, there is no answer from God, and things only get worse?

Some of these questions are the reasons why people sometimes leave church, faith, and even religion all together. Like I said in the parable of the "High Wire Walker," if there is no difference in Suffering and Death since this Jew named Jesus from Nazareth came, then why should any one believe in Him as a loving God?

St. James said in his Epistle,

☐ *"You ask, but you don't receive, **because you ask wrongly**." (James 4:3)*

This Scripture passage from the Epistle of James gives you the answer as to why God sometimes does not answer your prayers. The reason why is, *"You ask wrongly."* He goes on to say what is wrong about the way we ask.

☐ *"Yet even when you do pray, your prayers are not answered, because you pray just for selfish reasons." (James 4:4)*

Let's take this and apply the **Life is School** paradigm.

ANALOGY and ANSWER:

If you went to college after high school, did you select the college you ultimately attended **on the condition that Admissions would let your parents live with you all four years?** I bet not. Well then, let me ask you another question. Why wouldn't you want your parents who clothed you, fed you, and did everything for you to be your roommates?

My guess is that your answer goes something like this:

- ☐ I want to be independent.
- ☐ I want to make my own decisions.
- ☐ I want to do what I want to do.
- ☐ I want to choose my own future.
- ☐ I don't want anybody telling me what to do and what not to do.
- ☐ I want to make my own rules and life.

Does the above sound like reasons you would give **NOT** to have your parents live with you for four years?

THE ANSWER TO WHY GOD ALLOWS SUFFERING

Because Life is School, and you are to learn by making your own decisions, it's up to you to make them and be responsible for them.

- ☐ Right or Wrong
- ☐ Good or Evil
- ☐ Selfish or Generous
- ☐ Love or Hate
- ☐ Gods Will or My Will
- ☐ Forgive or Punish
- ☐ Sacrifice or Abuse
- ☐ Lie or Tell the Truth
- ☐ Look out the window or Pay attention
- ☐ Help others or Help yourself
- ☐ To give or Be greedy
- ☐ Respect or Disrespect
- ☐ Lust or Loving relationship
- ☐ Despair or Trust
- ☐ Do your work or Have somebody else do it.

The last decision is the reason God allows suffering. This is the same reason you didn't want your parents being your roommates in college, because you wanted to make your own decisions and choices and not have your parents tell you what to do. **Bingo!** There's the answer. **YOU** are in school, not your parents. You have to learn now, pay attention, and do your own homework. The quizzes, the tests, the exams are yours—not your parents'. Your problems in life are yours, not your parents'. And it is you who has to learn what to do and how to do it.

Are you getting the point here? When you pray and ask the Lord to take away your problems and suffering, and you think He doesn't answer, He's simply saying that you will never learn how to **TRUST** and deal with your problems "if I write your papers for you, take your tests, and do your labs." All these are opportunities for you to learn to Trust and make the necessary choices. If God did everything for you, you would not learn anything; however, if you choose to listen to Him, He will give you the power and know how to conquer your problems and struggles in life. That power, as we have learned, is Him being **with** us when we go through them.

<u>STOP</u>:
Take a moment to really read this part over, and replace your long held belief that God is supposed to answer all of your prayers and give you what you ask for. He wants you to Trust Him, which is what we are to receive our diploma in. When we ask for selfish reasons and for God to do every thing we ask, that is what the Scripture is referring to as asking **WRONGLY**. What we need to do is pay attention to the Teacher, the Lord, what He said, teaches us to do, and how to do it.

By now, you may be questioning why the word TRUST is being repeated so often. Well, how many times did you have to say the alphabet before you memorized it, or write 500 times: "I will not talk in class"?

So, every once in a while I will be repeating the following steps on How to Trust, because I want you to keep reading them until you memorize them and are able to do it automatically. Remember, as I said, Trust is the key that unlocks the door to the Truth, and more importantly to experiencing the Lord, His Unconditional Love, Forgiveness, and Healing.

Take your time and read them again, start to memorize them, and then do your homework by practicing. Don't be distracted by boredom, looking out the window, or telling yourself that you don't need to do it because you understand it. The Lord does not want you to only understand. He wants you to remember the High Wire Walker parable, get in the wheelbarrow, and get off the bleachers.

HERE ARE THE STEPS TO TRUST AGAIN

No matter what thoughts are in your mind, and no matter how intense your feelings and emotions are

1. **Choose** (*use your Will*) to focus off of them, the problem, the fear, and what is tempting you.

2. **Focus** on Jesus with you by simply saying "Lord."

3. **Keep choosing** to stay focused and say **NO** to your negative thoughts, feelings and emotions.

4. **Rest** in His presence, whether you feel Him or not, until you find Peace of Mind.

5. **Replace** your negative thoughts, half-truths, and lies that are in your mind causing your fears, worries, and stress with the Truth and presence of the Lord.

6. Then **do** His will no matter what you think or feel, consistently aware that He is with you, giving you strength and power to deal with anything.

WHY DO SOME PEOPLE SUFFER MORE THAN OTHERS?

I don't know about you, but over the years as a priest, it really stinks to watch a family member or friend suffer and sometimes suffer horrifically. Years ago, I became so angry with God about it that I had it out with Him. I was sick and tired of going into hospitals and walking into a room and seeing family members crying, frightened, and feeling powerless as they watched their child, mother, father, loved one dying and in agony. There I stood with my great words of hope and healing: "You just have to have faith." I said a few prays and left. I always left angry, frustrated, and felt that the Lord was powerless, and I only aggravated the situation by implying that they didn't have enough faith.

So I had it out with the Lord. I told Him that I was never going to go into those situations until He gave me the answers to Suffering, Death, and told me the right things to do and say that would really help the person and family to experience healing and hope.

You are learning everything the Lord has revealed and taught me and is now teaching you. He answered my prayer, transformed my life and thinking, and I have strived to spread His word. I have watched him give hope to thousands, and I mean thousands of people, especially those who have been devastated by life.

Why do some people suffer more than others is a very real and important question for all of us who listen to the news every day and experience this unfair distribution of pain and misery.

THE ANSWER:

Let's apply our Life is School paradigm with Trust as the key and goal to the Truth and the Lord.

If life is school, and our earthly bodies are the school building, then my **SCHOOL** and **LIFE** are different from everybody else's. In addition to this, my program and lesson plan are different and built for me personally. In education, there are different models for how each of us to comprehend and learns according to our needs.

Given this, that is why some students are challenged more than others, but the goal is always the same— not to fix them or do the work for them, but to apply what they have learned to overcome any obstacles. **(TRUST)**

> ☐ *His master replied, "Well done, good and faithful servant! Because you have been faithful in a very small matter, you shall have authority over ten cities." (Lk. 19:17)*

What Jesus is teaching us here is to grow in Trusting Him. If you can trust Him when tempted by despair, you will grow in leaps and bounds and experience the Unconditional Love and Peace of God in the midst of the chaos in your suffering the way Jesus did, on the cross.

- "Father, why have you forsaken me?" Then Jesus' next words were a choice and act of His WILL, not His thoughts or feelings.
- "Father, into your hands, I commend my Spirit." (Lk. 23:44-49)

Let's reflect on this for a moment, because this is the moment of our salvation— the moment of our forgiveness and the moment of our gateway to eternal life that looks beyond death.

- *In agony, Jesus was frightened that He was dying, and this was the end of His existence.*
- *Jesus felt abandoned by His Father who was certainly not delivering Him from the cross.*
- *Satan and Evil now had Jesus in the flesh, on his turf and could do to Jesus' body and mind what He had and continues to do to ours, and that is to tempt and destroy us with doubt, despair, Suffering and Death.*

THIS IS THE KEY to answer all of our questions as to why some people suffer more than others do.

Jesus, with His last breath, makes an act of **TRUST**, and in doing so **CONQUERS** His fear of Suffering and Death at the end of his human life.

This is the goal of God sending us to school in these earthly bodies. How do we know that? **POP QUIZ:** What was the last thing Jesus said after "Father, into your hands I commend my Spirit"?

"It is accomplished." (Jn. 19:30)

What did Jesus accomplish? He did not escape the cross. He did not escape the excruciating horrific physical pain of the cross. He did not escape suffocation and the coldness of death creeping up His body at the end. He wasn't even able to block out the Evil, negative, half-truths and lies that were attacking Him, and with them—Fear, Horror, Doubt, and Despair.

BUT the Lord, the Son of God, our Savior and our Friend, had overcome our Fear and His'—the fear of Suffering and Death—by **TRUSTING** in the Unconditional Love of the Father. **AND NOW WE CAN.**

If Life is School, and our individual curriculums are all different, when I compare my experience of suffering with others who suffer horrifically, they go to Harvard or MIT and are on the cross with Jesus. As for me— I'm still in grammar school. Their tests and exams are a lot worse than mine, but if they, like Jesus, make a choice to Trust in the Lord in spite of the overwhelming temptation to succumb to Fear and Despair, then they have passed their final exams and have gotten their diploma with a Summa Cum Laude award. They graduate to the many mansions in Heaven.

"Each person will be rewarded according to his or her deeds."

"No more teachers, no more books, no more teachers' dirty looks."

Remember this jingle on the first day of summer vacation?

JESUS:

☐ *Do not let your hearts be troubled, trust in God, and trust in me. In My Father's house, there are many dwelling places. If it were not so, would I have told you that I am going to prepare a place for you? If I go and prepare a place for you, I will come back and welcome you into my presence, so that you also may be where I am. (Jn. 14:2)*

ST. PAUL:

☐ *All I want is to know Christ and to experience the power of his resurrection, to share in his suffering, and become like him in his death, in the hope that I myself will be raised from death to life. (Phil. 3:10)*
☐ *For I consider that **the sufferings** of the **present** are not worth being **compared** with the glory that is about to be revealed. (Romans 8:18)*
☐ *Therefore, we do not lose heart, but though our outer body is decaying, our inner spirit is being renewed day by day. For our suffering and affliction is temporary (school), and producing for us an eternal home (graduation-new life), and a glory far beyond all comparison.*
☐ *So we do not look at the things, which are seen (things of the world and physical reality- pleasure, entertainment, power, money, possessions), but at the things which are not seen (Jesus with and in us). For the things, which are seen are temporal and passing away, but the things, which are not seen are eternal. (2 Cor: 4:18)*

Now, when I visit or see someone who is in physical and mental agony, I know what to do, what to teach, and more importantly, what to tell them they can do, how to do it, and then do it with them to experience the Lord's Unconditional Love. The Lord's words and teachings really work, give great hope and an unbelievable future that awaits each of us when we leave our bodies, graduate, and go Home.

> ☐ *There is no fear where love exists. Rather, perfect love banishes fear, for fear involves punishment, and the person who lives in fear has not yet experienced love. (1 Jn. 4:18)*

WHAT TO DO ABOUT FEAR

Love then is what dispels FEAR. And that is how to conquer your fear of Suffering, problems, and Death. As long as you are still afraid, you haven't been set free by the experience of love. Most likely, because your attention and focus is on the problem *(the boo boo, cut and blood when you were out playing in the yard and had not yet called for Mommy).*

Did you know that Jesus and the Scripture said almost one hundred times, "Do not be afraid or let your hearts be troubled?" Fear and Worry are two of the greatest obstacles that are keeping you from the answers, the power and the love of God in Jesus. The good news is that now you know what to ask for and how.

Praise You, Jesus! Do I hear an AMEN?

Now, when I see people who are suffering more than me, after I finish praying with them, I say to Jesus, "Lord, I know that their reward in Heaven will be great, because of the extreme pain they are going through, and yet they still Trust in You. Give them a great mansion and place with You in Heaven. They deserve it. Meanwhile, I'll settle for a sleeping bag in the woods by a stream, given the minor tests and exams in my life **(school)**.

A PERSONAL STORY TO FIND PEACE OF MIND

My uncle Tony was lying on a hospital bed in the middle of his living room at home, in pain and dying. Uncle Tony was not my biological uncle, but I chose him to be my sponsor for Confirmation, because he was one of my favorite uncles. He was a real man of faith and brought me and my cousins to church all of the time, completing novenas, the Rosary, Stations of the Cross on Fridays, and Mass on Sundays.

When I came in and sat down next to him, he smiled and said he was glad to see me. I asked him how he was doing and if he was afraid. To this day, I will never forget what he said and the experience I had of the Lord right there with and in Him. He said, "No Francis, I'm not afraid. I've trusted the Lord my whole life, and He got me through every thing. No, Francis, I'm not afraid, because all I have to do is TRUST HIM **ONE MORE TIME**."

There it was, right in front of me in my Uncle—Peace of Mind, courage and waiting to go home. Then, with his Italian wit, he said, "The only thing I wish (and it's frustrating the hell out of me) is for this damn body to let me go." That's what we prayed for—that his body would die so that he could finally leave his school building, and graduate. And that he did, in peace, at one with his God.

SHORT QUIZ to see what grade you are in, when it comes to Inner Peace, like my Uncle Tony's trust in the Lord.

How do you know you have Inner Peace?

INNER PEACE

- ☐ If you can start the day without caffeine and can relax without liquor.
- ☐ If you can always be cheerful, ignoring aches and pains.
- ☐ If you can resist complaining and boring people with your troubles.
- ☐ If you can understand when loved ones are too busy to give you any time.
- ☐ If you can take criticism and blame without resentment.
- ☐ If you can conquer tension without medical help.
- ☐ If you can sleep without the aid of drugs.

Then, you are probably the family dog!

It's a joke. Relax! You can still have your coffee and a beer.

What grade do you think you are in when it comes to Trust and experiencing Peace of Mind?

You are probably still in Kindergarten, but don't be discouraged. You are still in school, and Jesus is still teaching you and giving you more opportunities to learn.

AN ADDED ATTRACTION FOR YOU: If you aren't experiencing Peace of Mind now, or whenever you are anxious and worried about many things, I have set up an appointment with Jesus for you below— a short 'meeting with Jesus Prayer', for Peace of Mind." You are welcome to take a break from reading, talk and listen to the Lord, or continue reading, and pray it later.

When you are panicked, Peace of Mind and Rest are a few seconds away

JESUS

Peace be with you. It's me, Jesus, your Lord and Friend. I have been waiting for you. So, take a deep breath and relax. I know you are overwhelmed again, and your thoughts and feelings are out of control. You are frightened of what is happening to you and worried about what might happen to you tomorrow and in the future.

You are trapped in a vicious circle in your mind, between your thoughts that are threatening you and turning your fear into panic and terror. Evil is attacking you again, as it did me on the cross. Evil is tempting you to doubt that I am with you. You fear your suffering will never end.

So, take another deep breath to calm down. **Now** *let me help you again, and together we will stop the vicious circle.*

Slowly **Repeat My Words** *and let them rest your mind and body, little by little, so you can focus on Me here with you.*

☐ Be Still and Know that I am God...	**Pause 10 sec**
☐ Be Still and Know that I am...	**Pause 10 sec**
☐ Be Still and Know...	**Pause 10 sec**
☐ Be Still...	**Pause 10 sec**
☐ Be...	**Pause 15 sec**

The anxiety you are experiencing is from the negative thoughts that have entered your mind. Thinking about them over and over is how the evil powers of Fear, Panic, Doubt and Despair are taking control of your Will, Peace of Mind, and possessing your attention. Be aware that I am right here with you.

So, what are the negative thoughts, half-truths and lies that are attacking you this time: That your problem will get worse? That you won't be able to endure the suffering down the road? That the pain will never end? Or are you worried about your family and loved ones?

THESE THOUGHTS ARE THE <u>REAL ENEMY</u>. Dwelling on them is taking you down the path to despair, panic, and making you anxious.

STOP IT. Stop letting Evil do this to you. Together, let's you and I deliver and cast out these evil thoughts that are attacking you. Trust me by praying and repeating these words:

- ☐ "Your power, Jesus, is greater than the powers of Evil and Lies that are attacking me."
- ☐ "In Your name, Jesus, and by the power of your blood, I bind and cast out Fear, Worry, Anxiety, Doubt and Despair.
- ☐ **"You have no power over me. I belong to Jesus."** *(Pause 15 sec.)*
- ☐ "Lord, I'm tired and surrender everything to You... Give me Peace of Mind and Rest!"

Now take a deep breath, close your eyes, and enjoy Peace of mind and rest. Just keep choosing to be here with me and think positive and good thoughts, like all the people who love you. Picture them one by one and remember what it feels like when you are with them. Take your time and enjoy their presence when you do.

(Take as much time as you need and enjoy the Lord and those who love you.)

Now, no more thinking, no more praying. Let's just BE together, Me with you, and you with Me. **(Pause 1 Min., close your eyes. Be still and at peace.)**

YOU DID IT!

If you are emotionally drained from this, take a nap, or do something that you enjoy. **DO IT** and **STAY IN THE PRESENT**. Leave your problems, fears and future up to me. Now remember I will be right here with you, **whether you are aware of me or not** just in case we need to deliver these evil thoughts again...

I love you...always have and always will! **I will never abandon you, so don't abandon Me."** Amen!

Besides meeting with Jesus yourself to find and experience His peace in the midst of chaos, you might think about sharing the above prayer with a loved one when they are overwhelmed, like I have with you. You have my permission to use the prayer and be an instrument of healing, peace, and hope.

CHAPTER 8:
JESUS' SCHOOL SUBJECT
UNCONDITIONAL LOVE

If you go back to Chapter 2's chart describing life as school, you will see the subjects we are to study and grow in.

Paying attention to your teacher, Jesus, and doing what He asks is extremely important if you really want to know what you're supposed to be working on and doing every day. He said, just in case you forgot, "**THY** will be done" not "**your** will for God be done." So, don't think you're a genius and a "know it all" - like I did – **READ AND MEMORIZE.**

Life is School, and the subjects I take are:

- ☐ **UNCONDITIONAL <u>LOVE</u>**
- ☐ **UNCONDITIONAL <u>FORGIVENESS</u>**
- ☐ **UNCONDITIONAL <u>GENEROSITY</u>**
  (Repeat five times)

Again - this is not a theology or Scripture course, but rather a training manual, prayer book, conversation, and experience of Jesus with you as you read and pay attention.

<u>UNCONDITIONAL LOVE</u>

<u>JESUS</u>:

You have heard these words before, words that I taught 2000 years ago. Well, as you read them, I am saying them to you personally, right now.

- ☐ *"I want you to love one another, "I want you to love one another, **as I loved you**." (Jn. 13:34)*
- ☐ *"Love God with your **whole** Mind, Body, and Soul." (Mt. 22:34-40)*
- ☐ *"Love your neighbor as you love yourself." (Mk. 12:31)*
- ☐ *"Greater love hath no one than to lay their life down for their neighbor." (Jn. 15:13)*

These instructions are not suggestions that are optional, as many people have interpreted them to be, because they require a lifetime of work and sacrifice. They even might interfere with your lifestyle and ideas of what love entails.

What exactly is it that I am offering you and all humankind? I am offering you something greater than human love; and that is the Unconditional Love of your God and His Christ. Our Unconditional Love for you will not only transform your relationships, but transform your minds— the way you think about your God, others, and life. You will discover that you, everyone around you, even Creation itself are all connected by this Unconditional Love.

If you have not experienced My love, then this is something that you believe in but cannot quite make sense of, because you have not felt your connection to Me, others, and all of Creation.

***Relax**, Friend. Do not feel guilty or that you have done something wrong. You have not. Remember, you are still in school and there will be plenty of opportunities for you to experience My Unconditional Love for you. That's why I revealed to Francis, my co-author, to name this book, <u>The Most Important Book You Will Ever Read</u> because the purpose is for you to personally experience Me, right here with you, as you read. If you seek my embrace, like you did when you ran to your mother when you were a child, then close your eyes and imagine that I am giving you a Divine hug right now, because I am.*

All you have to do right now is, "Ask and you will receive. Seek, and you shall find. Knock, and the Door will open." I'm waiting...

Take a moment, close your mind and open your heart. Who knows what the Lord will do?

I remember the first time I experienced the Unconditional Love of the Lord and the Holy Spirit. For those who have, there are no human words to describe it, RIGHT? I really sought and asked for the Lord to let me experience and feel it. It did not happen for many years, but when it did, I realized it happened when I was ready.

Experiencing the Holy Spirit is only the beginning of the relationship Jesus wants with you. I spoke of this in Chapter 2 about how the transforming experience of Unconditional Love leads to a consistent dialogue with Jesus. The relationship with the Lord changes the way you think, make decisions, and live your life.

As co-author with Jesus, my contribution is the result of my own life in school with Jesus as my Teacher, Lord, and most of all, my best Friend.

That is why I gave Him first billing on the front cover, because as He was, and is for me now, He is for you.

Thank you, Lord, and thank you, Reader and Friend. Amen.

Now back to the subject of Unconditional Love.

- ☐ You cannot give what you do not have.
- ☐ You cannot teach what you were never taught.
- ☐ You cannot share and experience what you have never experienced yourself.

This is why we are in school, and why we need to learn what Unconditional Love is, how to experience and do it.

What is wrong with human love? Why do we need to learn how to love unconditionally? It is for the same reason we needed to learn how to read and write or learn English and arithmetic in school. God sent us here in the flesh to learn, prepare us for eternal life, and become what God created us to be.

Let us start by discussing the difference between human and Unconditional Love. When I give talks on this subject, I explain it this way. I ask people in the audience if there is a couple who owns a dog. When they raise their hand, I go over to them to introduce them and then ask what the name of their dog is.

Let's say it's "Duke."

I look at the wife and say, "When you get home tonight, I want you to lock Duke in the trunk of the car for three hours." She immediately says *No way*. "I'm telling you to lock Duke in the trunk of the car for three hours. After the three hours, unlock the trunk and let him out. When Duke sees you, his tail will start wagging, right? Then he will jump up and start licking you, won't he?" The wife smiles and says Yes. Then, pointing to her husband, I tell her to put her husband in the trunk of the car for three hours. **GET IT?**

That's the difference between human and Unconditional Love. One time when I was in New Jersey and did this at the end of the talk, the husband slipped the car keys out of his wife's purse. *(True story)*

JESUS:

"Love is patient, love is kind. It does not envy, it does not boast, it is not proud. It does not dishonor others, it is not self-seeking, it is not easily angered, and keeps no record of wrongdoing. Love does not delight in Evil, but rejoices with the truth. It always protects, always trusts, always hopes, and always perseveres. Love never fails." 1 Cor. 13:4-8

I really have no intention to describe Unconditional Love any better than the Word of God above. I do believe, however, that actions speak louder than words. Why? The goal for all of us is to **see** and **experience** the Unconditional Love of God.

So, take a minute or two and look deeply at a crucifix. Look beyond the horrific suffering that Jesus is going through and ask to experience the love that is driving Him, moment by moment, to endure it.

(Pause and imagine the Lord is embracing you, because He is.)

The disciple John was right when he wrote the following in his Epistle, *"**God is LOVE** and anyone who loves and knows God, for God is in them, and they are in GOD." (1 Jn. 4:19-27)*

This is why we love God, because He loved us first and continues to do so. His goal, while we are here in school, is to teach us not only about Unconditional Love but to experience and do it.

So, here it is again: how to do it, and of course, it is by TRUSTING. Take your time, and imagine doing each step in your mind. This will retrain your mind and will ultimately lead you to choose to sacrifice what your human side wants to do, and LOVE instead.

STORYTIME: JIM AND JEN

One afternoon when I was giving a series of talks in a church, the pastor asked me to visit a woman (Jen) who was essentially a recluse that suffered a massive stroke five years prior.

So I knocked on the door and was greeted by an elderly man named

James, about 82 years of age. He immediately led me to his wife who was in the center of the living room in a hospital bed. When I introduced myself, she was unable to respond because of her stroke. As Jim and I talked, I noticed several books on the bed stand, a crucifix, prayer book, and a rosary. He told me with a smile that Jen liked it when he read to her. He went on to tell me that they prayed and said the rosary in the morning and just before bedtime. All the time he was talking, he held his wife's hand and gently caressed it.

When I left, he walked me to the door. That's when I asked him if he had a nurse or someone come in to help him feed, wash, and change her. No, was his response, and he said that he was fine doing all those things himself for Jen. The thought of Jim doing this for five years blew me away. Then I asked him if it was frustrating and exhausting. With a smile, he looked back to the room where his wife was and said *She's a grand ol' gal, my wife, and she would do the same for me if I was in that bed.*

I knew and felt the Unconditional Love of God in this man named Jim and in his wife, Jen.

SUMMARY:

- God is Unconditional Love.
- Unconditional Love is what Heaven is like and what will bond us with God and each other, like Jim and Jen.
- If this story does not define, explain, and tell you what and how to do it, then nothing will. Now that you understand, the Lord is waiting to help you choose to do it. So keep your spiritual eyes open for the Lord to give you opportunities to sacrifice and love others as He loved you.

STEPS TO UNCONDITIONAL LOVE

- Focus and learn to be aware of people around you who are suffering, in need, or in harm's way.
- Experience a deep compassion the more you are focused on the victim or person suffering.
- Become aware of the Lord with you and His words, "Love one another, as I have loved you" and "Greater love has no one than to lay their life down for a friend."

- Then do His will, constantly aware that He is with you giving you strength and power to deal with your fear and danger
- The essential element in Unconditional Love is a willingness to sacrifice ones life, safety and wellbeing for the sake of another's.
- "Into Your hands I commend my Spirit"

STOP: As this chapter ends, take time to ask the Lord from your heart to grant you the grace to love others the way He unconditionally loves you.

PRAYER OF ST. FRANCIS

Lord, make me an instrument of your peace;

Where there is hatred, let me sow love;

Where there is injury, pardon;

Where there is doubt, faith;

Where there is despair, hope;

Where there is darkness, light; and

Where there is sadness, joy.

O Divine Master, grant that I

May not so much seek to be consoled as to console,

To be understood as to understand,

To be loved as to love.

For it is in giving that we receive,

It is in pardoning, that we are pardoned,

And it is in dying, that we are born to eternal life.

AMEN.

You will learn more specific ways to love unconditionally in the following chapters.

CHAPTER 9:
JESUS' SCHOOL SUBJECT:
UNCONDITIONAL FORGIVENESS

LET'S CONTINUE TO PRAY as we begin on the second subject we take while we're in school— Unconditional Forgiveness.

Lord, this strikes at the core of my life. Forgiveness is one of the main reasons You came to save us. Temptation and Sin are Satan and Evil's greatest weapons to distract, control, enslave, and destroy us.

Teach me, Lord, how to forgive others, even my worst enemy and those who crucify and commit horrific crimes: terrorists, murderers, or rapists.

Lord, forgive me my sins, as I forgive those who sin against me.

- ☐ **Response.** *"Lord, help me."*
- ☐ *For the grace to forgive others, even my enemies...* **Lord, help me**.
- ☐ *For the grace to forgive myself and let you free me from guilt and self-hatred...R.*
- ☐ *For the grace to not hold onto grudges, anger, and hatred...R.*
- ☐ *For the grace to speak the truth whenever I encounter Evil and Sin...R.*
- ☐ *Lastly, increase my strong desire to learn how to forgive my enemies and the worst of sinners, no matter how evil or grave their sin is.R.*
- ☐ *AMEN.*

FORGIVENESS

DO YOU HAVE ANSWERS AND SOLUTIONS?

- ☐ Have you said, thought, or done things you are ashamed of?
- ☐ Do you commit the same sins over and over again, no matter how hard you try not to?
- ☐ When you sin, do you feel like a hypocrite when you go to church?
- ☐ Do you punish yourself with self-hatred when you sin? "I'm a sinner, and there is no forgiveness for me."
- ☐ Have guilt and fear kept you from admitting your sins and going to Confession?
- ☐ Do you forgive your enemies whether they ask or not?
- ☐ Do you hold onto anger, grudges, and want to punish people who hurt you?
- ☐ Could you forgive someone who hurt you deeply— a terrorist, murderer, or rapist? Jesus expects you to forgive

them, but are you willing to learn how?

☐ Do you feel that God may not forgive you, and you may be going to hell?

JESUS:

☐ I say, love your enemies, do good to those who hate you, pray for those who persecute you.

☐ Forgive, not just seven times, but seven times seventy.

TRIUMPH OVER EVIL AND SIN

To understand Forgiveness, we need to understand Evil, Sin, and how they infect our minds with negative thoughts, half-truths, lies, temptation and seduction.

We learned earlier that Satan and Evil can only put thoughts and images in our minds and can only influence our Will and Conscience if we choose to allow it by dwelling on them. Doing this fuels our fears, passions, desires, and emotions. Then the more we dwell on these thoughts and images—lust, self-righteousness, hatred, pride—the promise of pleasure drives us to act on them. Now we are in total warfare between Good and Evil, and our Minds are the battlefield.

We do not live in a vacuum, but in a world with others in society. We are surrounded every day by a ton of ideas about what's right, wrong, legal, illegal, good and bad. Where are they, you ask? They are in the media, email, religion, movies, billboards, advertisements, teachers, family, friends, and everyone we meet. Because we have been trained to download everything without consciously knowing it, we have downloaded the virus of Evil that affects our conscience, moral compass and our choices to do what is right and what is wrong.

A QUICK REMINDER of what we learned about **conscience**. It warns, judges, and blames. A developed conscience is like a compass that directs us to what is right and good.

Culture and society's morals are constantly threatened by Evil for the sole purpose of destroying us and using us to destroy each other.

THE DETERIORATION OF RIGHT, WRONG, AND CONSCIENCE

Allow me to give you my analysis of what has happened to the moral compass of our society and around the world for the past 50-60 years.

I find that the evolution of the NIKE logo since the 60s describes the deterioration of objective truth in our society.

In the 60s came the sexual and anti-institutional movement. Everything was challenged, especially morality.

- **1960s NIKE**: *If it FEELS Right, Do It*
  What was Right is no longer determined by objective Truth, how it benefits the individual, others, society. This does not just include immediate gratification, but long term.
  Now, "my feelings" determine what Right is. This is a radical shift from objective truth and morality to subjective morality, determined by each person and their feelings.
- **1970s-1990s NIKE**: *If it FEELS Good, Do It*
  The missing word now is **RIGHT** replaced by GOOD. There is no more need to do what is Right for my sake, others or society, rather what **FEELS** GOOD for me. Now, I have become the center of the Universe and God.
- **NEW MILLENIUM NIKE**: *Just DO IT*
  Nothing to do with Right, Wrong, or even how it feels.
- **PRESENT DAY NIKE**: "DO IT"
  It makes no difference if it feels good or not, just do it. And if you get caught, just lie and deny it. Why not?
  The main goal now, is to get whatever you want, no matter how you get it. Do whatever you want and forget about how it affects anybody around you, directly or indirectly. "No one can tell me what to do; it's my right and my life." "I give myself the RIGHT and am accountable to no one— not God, not the law, not anybody." Sound familiar?

The more people have devolved into this way of reasoning and behaving, the more their **CONSCIENCE** dies and no longer warns, judges, or blames. That is why we recoil from the Evil done by some people and say, "How could they do such a thing? It's Evil and Demonic!" The Truth is, it is EVIL. Now you know why and how it gradually influences, controls, possesses, and then destroys us and others along the way.

FORGIVING OTHERS

STORYTIME: On October 2006, a 32-year-old milkman named Charles Roberts walked into an Amish school in Lancaster county and shot 10 young girls, killing five of them before killing himself. Only a few hours after the shootings the Amish community reached out to the killer's parents, the Roberts. Some of their Amish neighbors came to the Roberts' door.

One of the Amish men wrapped his arms around Charles' dad and said, "We will forgive your son." Rev. Lefever, the Roberts' pastor who witnessed this said this at Charles' funeral, "God walked in into the Roberts' kitchen and met us through the Amish neighbor's forgiveness. Their remarkable lack of bitterness, hatred, their refusal to retaliate or demand vengeance, offers a message from Jesus: **Forgiveness heals both the forgiver, as well as the forgiven.**"

Some of the girls' parents and many others of the Amish community attended Charles Roberts' funeral, their children's murderer. Charles' mother, Terri Roberts said, "There are no words to describe how they made us feel the day of our son's funeral, for the mother and father who had lost, not just one, but two daughters at the hand of our son, to come up and be the first ones to greet and embrace us at our son's funeral… Is there anything in this life that we and all of us should not forgive?"

While thousands across the country said the killer's ashes belonged in a trash barrel and that he should rot in hell, the Amish spoke differently and said that Charles was "overcome by Evil, but he was not an evil man."

HOW DO WE FORGIVE OTHERS

1. **CHOOSE TO FOCUS AWAY**
   From negative thoughts, images and feelings

2. **FOCUS ON JESUS**,
   His words and how He did it

3. **CHOOSE TO ABSORB**
   The horrific thoughts, images, and devastating darkness with an awareness and focus on Jesus with you. **Forgive the person.**

The Amish followed these steps, did not give in to hatred, revenge, or judging. Instead, they trusted the Lord and forgave the man who murdered their children. **That is UNCONDITIONAL FORGIVENESS**.

For those of you thinking "That may be wonderful for the Amish, but that isn't going to do it for me. And I'm not going to forgive anybody who killed or raped my daughter. I don't care what Jesus said, they deserve to die and be sent to Hell."

If you have these thoughts and are still tempted to have them, then it is important to examine them and figure out where they are coming from and what to do about them. They are what is keeping you from forgiving unconditionally, which is what we are supposed to learn how to do while we are here in school. These thoughts, feelings, and way of thinking are from Evil.

DON'T PANIC & THINK·THAT YOU ARE NOT TO HOLD EVIL ACCOUNTABLE.

JESUS:

- *Yes, I am merciful and quick to forgive, but I am also a Just God and hold each one accountable for their actions. That is why I confronted the religious leaders, because of how they let Evil corrupt them with power and wealth.*
- *But woe to you, Scribes and Pharisees, hypocrites, because you shut off the Kingdom of Heaven from people; for you do not enter in yourselves, nor do you allow those who are entering to go in. Woe to you, Scribes and Pharisees, hypocrites, because you travel around on sea and land to make one proselyte; and when he becomes one, you make him twice as much a son of hell as yourselves.*
- *Woe to you, Scribes and Pharisees, hypocrites! For you tithe mint and dill and have neglected the weightier provisions of the law: justice and mercy and faithfulness; but these are the things you should have done without neglecting the others. You blind guides who strain out a gnat and swallow a camel!*
- *Woe to you, Scribes and Pharisees, hypocrites! For you clean the outside of the cup and of the dish, but inside they are full of robbery and self-indulgence.*
- *Woe to you, Scribes and Pharisees, hypocrites! You are like whitewashed tombs, which on the outside appear beautiful, but inside they are full of dead men's bones and all uncleanness. So you,*

91

too, outwardly appear righteous to men, but inwardly you are full of hypocrisy and lawlessness.

☐ *You serpents, you brood of vipers, how will you escape the sentence of hell?*

<u>WHOA</u>! This is not the **Nice "Gentle" Jesus.**

So, what are you saying, Lord?

When it comes to Forgiveness, we need to know and understand the difference between

☐ **FORGIVENESS**
☐ **ACCOUNTABILITY & JUSTICE**
☐ **JUDGMENT**

<u>FORGIVENESS</u>: To focus off of what a person has done and the pain and damage they have caused, then focus on them as a person and offer them the opportunity to admit, own, repent, commit to change with a desire to reconcile and restore the relationship.

<u>ACCOUNTABILITY</u>:

Just saying "I'm Sorry" doesn't cut it. Anybody can say "I'm sorry" and think that everything they are saying and doing is OK. To those people who think this way, **IT'S NOT OK.** All that "I'm Sorry" says to me is that you got caught and are trying to exonerate yourself from any guilt or responsibility for what you have done. Lastly, "I'm Sorry" does not contain any verbal admission or behaviors that express remorse and ownership of the damage you have done. In addition to this, these two words say nothing about your commitment to change or a desire to heal and restore the relationship. The choice to forgive, heal and reconcile belong to the victim, not the person who says "I'm Sorry."

☐ Repent
☐ Change
☐ Reconcile

<u>JUDGMENT</u>: **Condemnation or Salvation; Heaven or Hell?**

This is why, **JUDGMENT** is not ours to do, no matter who a person is or what they are doing.

<u>JESUS</u>: **"Do not Judge lest ye be judged."**

Knowing the difference between forgiveness, accountability and judgment can help in unconditionally forgiving others. Knowing that we can hold those who have hurt us accountable gives us a   ʼ **PATH** to follow.

<u>WHAT TO DO ACCORDING TO JESUS</u>:

<u>JESUS</u>:

1. If your brother or sister sins, go and point out their fault, *just between the two of you.*

2. If they listen to you, you have won them over. But, if they will not listen, take one or two others along, so that "every matter may be established by the testimony of two or three witnesses."

3. *If they still refuse to listen, tell it to the church, and if they refuse to listen even to the church, treat them as you would a pagan or a tax collector. (Mt. 18:15-17)*

<u>ACCOUNTABLITY</u>

"You, wicked servant," Jesus said. "I canceled all that debt of yours, because you begged me to. Should you not have had mercy on your fellow servant, just as I had on you?"

In anger, the Master handed him over to the jailers to be tortured, until he should pay back all he owed.

This is how my Heavenly Father will treat each of you unless you forgive your brother or sister from your heart. (Mt. 18)

Did you ever have someone judge you falsely and failed to confront you face to face? Instead, they tell someone above you or make it public, and of course, they remain anonymous. Then, what makes it worse is, they hide behind self-righteousness and their interpretation of what Jesus said to fit their narrative and what they want. If you have experienced this, perhaps you feel like retaliating.

It is anger and self-righteousness that wants to retaliate. They are the main factors from keeping you from forgiving. It is important to understand anger and how Evil uses it to destroy not only the person who has wronged you, but mostly yourself in the process.

ANGER THAT IS NOT SINFUL
Jesus was angry several times as we learned from what He said to the Pharisees and the religious leaders. But He confronted them face to face, pointed out their sins, told them the truth, what to do, and what not to do. Jesus is telling us that if we have anything against someone, we should go to them and point out their wrongdoing, tell them the truth, and help them to change their ways.

ANGER THAT WANTS TO RETALIATE IS SINFUL
Anger that wants to punish is your sin. When you focus only on what a person is doing and dwell on it, anger enters and stokes up your emotions. The more you think about what someone is doing, the more you desire to hurt and cause pain to that person.

Then we think about ways to punish the person, and with these thoughts comes self-righteousness that drives us to do it with the promise that we will feel good and justified later. This kind of anger leads to hatred and violence. What makes this a sin is that it destroys us by becoming obsessed and an unhappy person.

My brother described this kind of anger best when he said, "It's like me taking poison, waiting for you to die."

EXERCISE:

Think of someone you have not been able to forgive. In your mind, choose to go through the steps one by one. It may be difficult and even impossible for you because of the anger and self-righteousness that's controlling your thoughts, like *They deserve it; They should never be forgiven; I hope they rot in hell.*

Take your time and do battle with Evil in your mind, and let Jesus give you victory and peace. Apply the steps below in your mind, like the Amish did, to retrain your mind. It will be extremely difficult, but remember, you can't do 50 pushups until you can do one.

1. CHOOSE TO FOCUS AWAY from these thoughts, images, and feelings.

2. FOCUS ON JESUS, His Words and how He did it.

3. CHOOSE TO ABSORB THE PAIN THE PERSON CAUSED YOU NO MATTER WHAT. Then forgive the person, confront them with the truth, and offer ways to help them to stop doing it, no matter how intense your anger.

GOOD NEWS:

Forgiving, Jesus' way, not only can heal the person who sinned or wronged you, but it will liberate you from anger, put it to rest, and give you peace.

JESUS:

- *I unconditionally loved you, before you sinned, while you were sinning, and after you sinned.*
- *My love for you has and will never change. My only desire is to have you know and experience it.*

THE PARABLE OF THE PRODIGAL SON

There was a man who had two sons. The younger one said to his father, "Father, give me my share of the estate." So, he divided his property between them.

Not long after that, the younger son got together all he had, set off for a distant country, and there squandered his wealth In wild living. After he had spent everything, there was a severe famine in that whole country, and he began to be in need. So he went and hired himself out to a citizen of that country who sent him to his fields to feed pigs. He longed to fill his stomach with the pods that the pigs were eating, but no one gave him anything.

When he came to his senses, he said, "How many of my father's hired servants have food to spare, and here I am starving to death!" ***I will set out, go back to my father, and say to him, "Father, I have sinned against Heaven and against you. I am no longer worthy to be called your son; make me like one of your hired servants."*** *So he got up and went to his father.*

But while he was still a long way off, his father saw him and was filled with compassion for him; he ran to his son, threw his arms around him and kissed him.

The son said to him, "Father, I have sinned against Heaven and against you. I am no longer worthy to be called your son."

But the father said to his servants, "Quick! Bring the best robe and put it on him. Put a ring on his finger and sandals on his feet. Bring the fattened calf and kill it. Let us have a feast and celebrate. For this son of mine was dead and is alive again; he was lost and is found." So they began to celebrate. (Lk. 15:11-32)

I love this parable of Jesus, because it contains the revelation of God's Unconditional Love and Forgiveness in one. The key word here is Unconditional. What is this "Unconditional Love" like, when it comes to forgiveness for the prodigal son and us?

<u>**WELL, HERE IT IS:**</u>

After his father ran out to his son, when he saw him in the distance, the son said,

"Father, I have sinned against God and you. I no longer deserve to be your son. Treat me as one of your servants." (Lk. 15:11-32)

Pay careful attention to the Father's response.

"Put a ring on his finger, give him the best robe, kill the fatted calf and let's celebrate, for my son who was dead is alive again, lost but now he is found." (Lk. 15:11-32)

HIS RESPONSE IS UNCONDITIONAL LOVE AND FORGIVENESS.

And that was the new covenant (promise). Why?

HE NEVER ONCE ASKED HIM WHAT HIS SINS WERE, OR ON WHAT HE SPENT HIS INHERITANCE.

FORGIVENESS

OLD & NEW COVENANT

<u>**OLD COVENANT**</u>:

- ☐ Be perfect, keep the law, then God will love you.
- ☐ This is to be done by God's promise and not by animal sacrifices.

The sacrifices made under the law could not take away sins; it was impossible; and those sacrifices only pointed to the offering of Jesus' body and blood (Hebrews 10:1-18). Once He made that sacrifice, there was no longer any need for further sacrifices.

1. *God never took pleasure in the sacrifice of animals for the sins of the people, while they were under the law. These sacrifices could not make*

perfect the sinner seeking forgiveness through them.

2. *Those sacrifices did have a purpose. They served as a constant reminder of sins, and they pointed symbolically to the coming sacrifice (The Messiah) that could take away those sins.*

3. *The death of Jesus enabled "the redemption of the transgressions that were committed under the first covenant" (Hebrews 9:15). This was their faith and hope.*

4. *Their justification and forgiveness of sins rested on the promised Christ. They knew that goats could not take away their sins, but by faith in Christ, they could have their sins provisionally forgiven against the day that Christ would bring redemption.*

NEW COVENANT:

He unconditionally loves YOU, before, during, and after you sin!

HOW TO EXPERIENCE JESUS' FORGIVENESS in self-dialogue

FOCUS OFF:

The sin – Satan's lies keeping you from Jesus' forgiveness. He is infamously known as the Accuser.

- ☐ *I'm guilty, a hypocrite. God will never forgive me. I hate what I did, and I hate myself.*
- ☐ *I keep doing the same things, no matter how hard I try.*
- ☐ *God is going to punish me. I'm going to hell, and there's no hope.*
- ☐ *I hurt others deeply. I am responsible.*
- ☐ *I can never get back what I lost. God could never forgive me. I am embarrassed, ashamed, and just want to hide. This feeling of guilt will never go away, no matter what I do. I don't know if I can live with this for the rest of my life.*

FOCUS ON:

Jesus' Unconditional Love on the cross. Accept and experience it.

- ☐ *Jesus forgives and loves me anyway. He wants to free me and to forgive myself.*
- ☐ *My desire to change, do penance, to make up for my sins.*

His forgiveness is not free license to do whatever I want, because He will always forgive me. He forgives but expects me to be accountable, learn and change.

The Lord wants to know if you would like to let go of your sins, or anything that you have not yet put to rest. If you have anything that you have done that you regret and feel guilty about, here is an opportunity for you, now or later, to finally let the Unconditional Love Jesus had for you on the cross liberate you from Evil's plan to drag you down to self-hated and despair.

PAUSE:

AN UNCONDITIONAL FORGIVENESS PRAYER

EXAMINATION OF CONSCIENCE:

R: *Lord, forgive me.*

IF I HAVE:

- ☐ Not spent enough time every day, talking, listening, and just spending time with You... *Lord, forgive me.*
- ☐ Doubted that You care and were with me in my problems and suffering...*R.*
- ☐ Been impatient and mean-spirited...*R.*
- ☐ Judged people, gossiped, and even destroyed somebody's reputation...*R.*
- ☐ Lied, deceived, and stretched the truth to not get caught and take responsibility...*R.*
- ☐ Been jealous of other people, what they look like, and envious of their talents and abilities and wanted them for myself...*R.*
- ☐ Labeled and ignored people, because they are different...*R.*
- ☐ Not forgiven people, held a grudge, or wanted to punish them...*R.*
- ☐ Been cynical and a poor example to others...*R.*
- ☐ Used people for my own pleasure and gratification...*R.*

- ☐ Failed to be a good steward of my body, mind, and spirit, but instead watched and listened to TV, movies, music that influenced me toward violence and selfish pleasures.*R.*
- ☐ Had too much to drink or abused drugs...*R.*
- ☐ Abused nature, polluted the environment, or wasted the good things I have...*R.*
- ☐ Not fed the hungry, clothed the naked, cared for the sick, sheltered the homeless, or done anything to help people who are suffering...*R.*
- ☐ Thought, said, or done anything that disappointed You...*R.*
- ☐ Thought, said, or did anything that hurt someone. Heal them and forgive me...*R.*
- ☐ Not done your will, because I was too busy with my life and my own agenda...*R.*

ACT OF CONTRITION

"Jesus, have mercy on me. Forgive me, a sinner."

JESUS' ABSOLUTION

Does anyone condemn you? Then neither do I. Go now, and sin no more.

Close your eyes, sit still, and enjoy that you have been lifted from your guilt, shame, self-hatred, and are unconditionally loved by the God who created you, in Christ.

Alleluia!

CHAPTER 10:
JESUS' SCHOOL SUBJECT: <u>UNCONDITIONAL GENEROSITY</u>

The third subject we take while we are in school in our earthly bodies is Generosity. Your initial thoughts might suggest that this is the easiest of all to understand and do. Wrong! As you will learn, this is just as difficult as the other two and maybe even more. Generosity affects every aspect of our lives, especially our relationships. It has many enemies that, not only tempt, seduce, and drive us to destructive actions which cause division, and maybe even the greatest suffering to us all.

Let's jump in and get started by reflecting on Generosity. Let Jesus teach us what it is and how to do it.

<u>JESUS</u>:

The blessings you have received, give them freely.

If someone asks you for your coat, give them your cloak as well.

For I was hungry and you gave me something to eat. I was thirsty, and you gave me something to drink. I was a stranger, and you invited me in. I needed clothes and you clothed me, I was sick and you looked after me, I was in prison and you came to visit me.

Then the righteous will answer him, "Lord, when did we see you hungry and feed you, or thirsty and give you something to drink? When did we see you a stranger and invite you in, or needing clothes, and clothe you? When did we see you sick, or in prison, and visit you?" (Mt. 25:31-26)

The King will reply, "Truly I tell you, whatever you did for one of the least of these brothers and sisters of mine, you did for Me." (Mt. 25:35-40)

It seems clear that the Lord describes the **heart** of generosity.

For now, in His words above, He teaches that generosity is more than giving the basic human needs, but rather giving of our time, skills, gifts, and as Pope Paul VI said, "...not out of our excess, but out of our sustenance." That would represent a radical change in our thinking, attitude, and spirituality. It would translate into moving from our "safe zone," to unknown waters for the sake of learning and growing in Jesus' call to unconditional generosity.

Remember the parable of the "high wire walker"? Who said get into the wheelbarrow? Well, this is where Evil, Fear, and self-justification tempts and seduces us to stay on the bleachers where it's safe, rationalizing not getting into the wheel barrow, not doing what Jesus asks— resulting in our own destruction by being controlled by fear.

For the sake of safety and control, we are fixed in our own world by a false sense of security that keeps us from Jesus and His power instead of TRUSTING Him, staying focused on Him, and experiencing Him with us. I hope you are remembering the steps to TRUST, because here they are the answer for everything— in this case, Unconditional Generosity.

So what are the devastating results of a lack of generosity in our personal lives, our family, and in the world?

As I go around the country preaching and meeting thousands of people, I listen to their stories of faith, but mostly their stories of stress, frustration, disorder, unhappiness, and dissatisfaction in life— that no matter what they have been doing, there is still this emptiness that is never completely filled. This begs the question of, Is that all there is to life?

After a while, I started listing where all this Stress, Fear, Unhappiness and Emptiness are coming from. The following represents the vast majority of the stories from kids to seniors around the country.

JOBS: Not happy with what they are doing; who they are working with. Afraid of losing their job without finding a new one, and unable to support themselves and family.

BILLS: Taxes, insurances, mortgages, cell phones, internet, TV, travel, gasoline, utilities, food, clothing, tuitions, electronics, etc. Do I need to go further? I'm sure you have your own to add.

EVENTS AND ACTIVITIES: Attending sports events, games, parties, birthdays, anniversaries, showers, weddings, Baptisms, First Communions, transporting kids and grandkids to and from all their practices, games and activities.

After listening to the same stories over and over again, I started to admit that they were describing me, my life, identified my own stress, feelings of unhappiness, and even emptiness. Aren't we all waking up every day and just trying to be happy— to have a good day, hoping to find time for ourselves, doing what we want?

Given all the stress, unhappiness and dissatisfaction, my conclusion is that many today, even sisters and brothers of faith, from kids to seniors, are running around like maniacs trying to be happy. Instead, we experience more and more stressed out days and sleepless nights.

HOW THIS TRANSLATES INTO OUR LIVES

MARRIAGE: More and more conflicts in marriages, resulting in distancing, resulting is frustration, loneliness, then possible divorce.

Sixty percent of marriages end in divorce and with the devastating effects on children.

SINGLES & SINGLE PARENTS: All the above mentioned. Jobs, bills, except no one to share them with for support and love. This causes stress and loneliness.

FAMILY: More and more disagreements in families with kids and parents involved in their own activities, wanting to do what they want to do, and when they want to do it. Little by little, they become self-centered and distanced from each other. Parents and other family members soon become the enemy, because they are restricting and denying them. In the end, they become simply individuals living in the same house, but far from being a family, because no one has a desire or need to create one.

KIDS: I find that many kids today are angry, unhappy, never satisfied, and especially bored. So where does their stress come from. After listening to thousands of kids, especially teenagers, I think their stress comes from home, the rules, restrictions, and chores they are responsible for. School is another stress by paying attention all day, doing drills, exercises, answering questions, and then homework.

I think most of kids' stress today comes from having to spend six hours a day in school listening to their schoolmates making fun of them, because of the way they look or don't look like, what they dress like or what they don't, what they have or what they don't have. Listening to the bullying causes the most stress. No wonder they want their iPods on, staring at a cell phone, involve themselves with sports and video games, and maybe even get involved in sex, drugs, etc. It's their only chance to "zone out" and escape the boredom, pain, and stress.

The real tragedy here that continues to sadden me is that all the things and activities they turn to, good or bad, are addictive. They also end with boredom and loneliness. The final tragedy for young people today is that they believe this is what life is about, and there is no other way.

VERY IMPORTANT FOR YOUNG PEOPLE

If you are in junior high, high school, or a young adult reading this, then read and re-read this chapter. You will not only get answers for many of your problems, frustrations, and boredom, but good news from Jesus that there is another way of thinking and living. The new way will lead you to real joy, happiness, and eternal life when your bodies end and you go home to where God created you. So, KEEP READING!

SENIORS: You don't have to tell me your stories to know where your stress is coming from. All anyone has to do is look at your faces. You are frightened about your health and your future, where will you live when you can no longer take care of yourself, who will take care of you, and how are you going to pay for it. Little by little, as your health deteriorates, you can no longer do those things you enjoyed doing your whole life. Then you lose your spouses, friends, and are isolated into a life of loneliness, waiting to die. THIS causes STRESS.

JESUS:

I have come to give you life and life to the fullest – Joy and make your Joy complete; peace, unlike the peace the world gives.

So, what's the question for Jesus who said "I have come to give you Life, Joy, and Peace?"

Given all the stress, fear, arguing, frustration, dissatisfaction and emptiness—

WHERE IS IT JESUS?

<u>THE ANSWERS</u>:

The **ANSWER** is "The Kingdom of God"

You probably heard that phrase before and perhaps even sermons about what it is (Heaven, where God dwells), the Holy Spirit or Christ's love in our hearts, and maybe even the Church. The good news is that Jesus is going to teach you how the Kingdom of God and the equation works, because as He said, "The Kingdom of God is at hand."

If you were hoping that the answer would be a "magic" pill solving all of your problems and those things that are causing you stress, fear, worry, unhappiness, and dissatisfaction, you are probably very disappointed. But, don't be too disappointed or despair, because remember you are still in school, and Jesus is your teacher who will show you the WAY to Life, Joy, and Peace in the midst of your confusion.

<u>THE WAY</u>:

If you read the many times Jesus spoke of and proclaimed the Kingdom of God, He speaks of it in opposition to the Kingdom of Man or sometimes He referred to it as the "flesh" or "world." If you read carefully to Jesus' words describing the two Kingdoms, you will hear Him specifically detailing what each consists of in our thinking and living *(actions-deeds)*.

The Kingdom of God and the Kingdom of Man are two opposite ways of <u>THINKING</u> and <u>LIVING</u>.

<u>STOP</u>: Time for a **DRILL**. Do not read any further until you memorize the above teaching. Repeat it until you don't need to read it. This is the heart of the answer and equation.

Both the Kingdom of God and the Kingdom of Man *(this includes women)*, are two opposite ways of thinking about God, life, others, and ourselves. Secondly, they are two very different ways of living *(our actions)*.

Let's begin with: **THE KINGDOM OF MAN**

In the beginning of this chapter, I spoke of the enemies of generosity. The underlying enemies of the Kingdom of God are Satan, Powers, Principalities, and Rulers of the Kingdom of darkness as we discussed in earlier chapters. As you read on, Jesus and I will expose them, how they operate, and what their plan is to control and destroy you.

Remember that Evil can only put thoughts and images in your mind. It's up to you to choose to dwell on them or not. If you do, this is how you let Evil in. The more you think about them, the more you will believe in them as the truth *(your thinking and beliefs)*.

Little by little we are all tempted and seduced to:

REPLACE **GOD** as the source for our Happiness, Joy, Life, and Fulfillment with our **DESIRES** for things and activities that promise us we will feel good, important, attractive, in control, comfortable, and entertained, when we own and have them. The **Kingdom of Man** sells, teaches, and tempts us with this way of thinking and living.

To expose Satan and Evil's subtle way of tempting, controlling, and addicting us to his way of thinking and living, please reflect upon chapter 6. Don't just read it this time, but examine your life to see the ways you have been tempted and seduced recently.

GOD:

I am the Lord thy God. Thou shalt not have strange Gods before Me. *(Ex. 20:7)*

When we are seduced and tempted to replace God with our human desires for things and activities and slowly get addicted to them, we are choosing the path that will lead to the destruction of ourselves, marriages, family, church, and in the bigger picture—our society. Like addicts, we will be in denial. Not a bad strategy for Satan and

Evil to not believe, and we offer no resistance while he is free to execute his plan for us and the world.

OUR DESIRES:

The ultimate threat to all of humanity is that our human desires are **INSATIABLE**.

The ultimate threat to all of humanity is that our human desires are **INSATIABLE**.

What do I mean by insatiable? It's obvious that no matter how many things, possessions I have, and no matter how many times I play sports, go shopping, or do all the activities I want to do, they never, and I mean, never, completely satisfy me. Rather, they leave me bored, lonely, empty, and most of all, dissatisfied.

That's why we always need more, more gadgets, electronics, the latest iPhones, bigger and better cars, the latest styles of clothing, wider TV screens, play on the school team, the recreation team, and if you are lucky, the travel team, and all at the same time. When you are not playing, you are bored and dissatisfied.

This is what Evil and the Kingdom of Man teaches that life and success are all about, and the pleasure we get from it is what addicts us. If you are in denial, and don't believe this, try taking a cell phone from a teenager!

You have read what I think and believe, now read where it came from.

> ☐ *Many, as I have told you in tears, conduct themselves as enemies of the cross of Christ. Their end is their destruction. Their god is their stomach. Their minds are occupied with earthly things, but our citizenship is in Heaven, and from there we await our Savior. (Phil. 3:18-21)*
> ☐ *Timothy, I tell you this. There will be terrifying times in the last days. People will be self-centered, lovers of money, proud, abusive, ungrateful, callous, slanderous and conceited. They will hate what is good, and be lovers of pleasure, rather than lovers of God, as they make a pretense of religion, but deny its power. (2 Tm. 3:1-5)*

WHAT TO DO ABOUT IT:

ACCORDING TO THE WORD OF GOD, AND NOT MINE

- *Strip yourselves of your former nature. Put off and discard your old un-renewed self, which characterized your previous manner of life and becomes corrupt through lusts and desires that come from delusion; and be constantly renewed in the spirit of your mind, having a fresh mental and spiritual attitude. (Eph. 4:22-23)*
- *Whatever gains I had, I now consider a loss because of Christ. Even more than that, I consider everything as loss, because of the extreme good of knowing Christ Jesus my Lord. (Phil. 3:7-8)*
- *The Grace of God has appeared, saving all and training us to reject godless ways and worldly desires, and live temperately and devoutly in this age as we await the blessed hope of our savior, Christ Jesus, our Lord. (Titus: 2:11-13)*

JESUS:

- *What good is it to inherit the whole world (things and possessions), and lose your very soul?*
- *You cannot serve God and money. You will love the one way of thinking and living, and despise the other. You will cling to one and hate the other.*
- *Do not store your treasure here where rust and moth can destroy it. Store your treasure in Heaven where there is no moth or rust to destroy.*

As a priest for many years and having seen thousands of funerals, I have yet to see a trailer hitch on a casket. Get it?

You will notice that I have not yet mentioned the word SIN when talking about the Kingdom of Man. All that I have said are good things, non-sinful activities and life styles. They are good, and God gave them to us to enjoy but **NOT** to replace Him with, serve or be addicted to them. Evil seduces us with them, because they are not sinful and do give us pleasure and fun, but Evil uses what is good to, little by little, commit our attention to focus on the gift, activity, and pleasure and not on the Giver, God.

Our addiction to the Kingdom of Man is more addictive and deadly than any opiate, heroin, cocaine, or synthetic drug.

Our focus and attention is on **THINGS** and **HAVING A RIGHT** to consume more and more with money to pay for them.

RESULTS: Life is all about **ME, ME, ME!**

These are some of the red flags that should go up if anyone might be getting enveloped into too much of the Kingdom of Man.

- ☐ "Gimme, Gimme, Gimme…"
- ☐ "I Want…"
- ☐ "I Need…"
- ☐ "I'll never ask for anything else…"
- ☐ "If I have that, I won't need anything else…"
- ☐ "It's my life. I can do whatever I want…"
- ☐ "Everybody else has one, why can't I…?"
- ☐ "I'm not doing anything wrong, so why can't I do it…?"

THE MENTALITY: We want it all and now.

This is the Original Sin. Appropriating God's power and Will to ourselves, and becoming our own god. Selfishness is how Evil has infected our minds and human nature. In this chapter on Unconditional Generosity, selfishness is the main enemy of generosity. The more we let selfishness dictate and control us, the more we will think, say, or do anything to get what we want. This is the evil path Satan wants to lead us down to lie, rob, cheat, rape, kill, torture, destroy from the smallest lie to a terrorist act in order to get what we want.

STORYTIME:

> There was a mother who had two daughters, Kara (six) and Lisa (four). The mother was making pancakes for breakfast. Kara and Lisa were arguing about who was going to get the first pancake. Their mother saw this as an opportunity to teach them about generosity. So, the mother told both of them, "If Jesus was here, He would say to give the first pancake to your sister."
>
> So, six-year-old Kara says, "Lisa, you be Jesus."

I'm sure you get the point. The same Evil behind Kara is the same behind a terrorist with different levels of will power to resist. Terrorists have been addicted and have become possessed to the point where they have no **conscience** and lost their **WILL**. They will do anything, no matter how horrific and demonic to get what they want, because of the pleasure and power it gives them. And it all began with selfishness and desire.

What is the Truth about living out of our desires? There are just too many things to do and want, and most of all, too great a price to pay.

WHY?

Because there is **NOT ENOUGH TIME** to have and do it all. **NO TIME** is the greatest obstacle to **GENEROSITY**. No time instead to

- [ ] **JUST BEING STILL** at peace with God, nature, and ourselves
- [ ] **CREATING, ENJOYING, BEING FAMILY** *(family becomes the enemy, because it seems they are controlling you and keeping you from being happy)*
- [ ] **EAT MEALS TOGETHER**, listening, understanding, loving and supporting each other
- [ ] **TALK & LISTEN** to be aware Jesus is with you, wanting to speak to you and reveal His will and plan for you throughout your day
- [ ] **GO TO CHURCH**, experiencing Jesus with our parish family.
- [ ] SERVE AND MINISTER the poor, sick, lonely, for and with our Church sisters and brothers

HOW THE KINGDOM OF MAN AFFECTS OUR FAITH

Before we get into how the Kingdom of Man affects our faith and lives, Jesus wants to remind you of a story He told about a young man, who asked Him for Eternal Life.

JESUS:

One day when I was setting out on a journey with my disciples, a man ran up and knelt before Me and asked, "Good teacher, what must I do to inherit eternal life?" So I said to him, you know the commandments, you shall not murder; you shall not commit adultery; you shall not steal; you shall not bear false witness; you shall not defraud; honor your father and mother." The young man said to me, "Teacher, I have kept all these since my youth." Then I looked at him with compassion and love, knowing what was in his heart, and what he really needed, and said, "There is still one thing left for you to do. Sell all that you have and distribute it to the poor, and then you will have treasure in Heaven. After you do this, then come back and follow me."

When the man heard this, he was shocked, and became very sad, and he left Me, for he had many possessions. So, as I told my disciples, "It's easier for a camel to pass through the eye of a needle than for a rich person to enter the kingdom of God." The young man had allowed himself to replace God with riches and possessions, and thought the Kingdom Of God was a THING he could purchase and own.

It cannot be that way with you. So listen and learn how to set yourself free, free to know and experience Me. Then I can walk daily with you and lead you to Peace of Mind and joy.

As Jesus said, the man thought Eternal Life was a **THING** he could purchase and own. **Wrong!** Jesus saw and knew exactly what he had become addicted to—money, things and possessions. Jesus also knew how Evil had deceived the man into believing that he had done enough to deserve eternal life (obeying the Commandments and the Law).

Listen carefully to this mentality that has plagued the Church and many parishes. Many believers have been seduced into believing that all you need to do to be a "good" Catholic is, be baptized, make your First Penance and Communion, get Confirmed, and go to church once in a while, as long as it doesn't interfere with your kids' schedules or yours.

HOW IT AFFECTS OUR FAITH:

- ☐ God becomes just another **thing to have**, and church another **thing to do.**
- ☐ We try to fit God into our life styles. **WRONG!** It's the other way around. We are called to fit our lives into God's.

"Thy kingdom come, Thy will be done."

STORYTIME (It's all about me and what I want)

- ☐ A middle-aged woman has a heart attack and is rushed to

110

the hospital. While on the operating table, she has a near death experience. During that experience, she sees God and asks if this is it.

□ God says *No* and explains that she has another 30 years to live. Upon her recovery, she decides to stay in the hospital and have a face-lift, liposuction, breast augmentation, tummy tuck, etc. She even has someone come in and change her hair color. She figures since she has another 30 years, she might as well make the most of it.

□ She walks out of the hospital after the last operation, is then run-over by an ambulance speeding by and dies. She arrives in front of God and complains. "I thought you said I had another 30 years."

□ God replied, "I didn't recognize you."

(C'mon, give me a break. Not one of these jokes, are mine.)

Church becomes just another thing I have to do to **get** God. When I'm there, I can't wait until it's over so I can do what I would rather be doing.

One of the ways I can tell if people in church are living out of their desires and the Kingdom of Man is that they are constantly checking their watches, waiting for me to shut up and get the service over so they can get to their game, tea time, breakfast, or go shopping.

Then I love those who come up to receive Communion, and the second they receive the Lord, they quietly sneak out the back door like zombies to avoid the traffic jam after the service and hurry to their first priority, what they want to do. The sad thing is they have no idea that they have been seduced.

The Kingdom of Man seduces us with money, power, entertainment and pleasure, promising us total satisfaction, fulfillment and success by having whatever we want as often as we want.

This mentality is rampant in the world, society, politics, religion, and in you and me. It is the enemy and always leads to spiritual death and even physical death.

EXAMPLES: OJ Simpson, Michael Jackson, Whitney Houston, Harvey

Weinstein, thousands upon thousands overdosed on drugs, and the list goes on and on.

THE POINT: They all had enough money to have whatever they wanted, do whatever they wanted and as often as they wanted to do it. Was this the path to fulfillment and satisfaction? When they lived this way, I'm sure they thought so, but living out of their desires promised them everything. In the end, it just led them to their own destruction, a victory and score for Evil.

KINGDOM OF MAN STORIES I HAVE HEARD AND SEEN

I OBSERVED A TEENAGER IN RELIGION CLASS, iPod and ear buds in, leg bobbing up and down to the music, texting on cell phone, talking to his friend sitting next to him, and all at the same time. Then we wonder why many suffer from attention spans. Oh, he at least looked up at his teacher every now and then, nodding his head to make her think he was listening.

A WOMAN CAME IN TO TALK TO ME and said her husband came home every day after work, watched TV sports all evening with a few beers, and went out with his buddies two and three nights a week, less and less time for her and the family. Then, he wondered why there was trouble with the marriage and the kids.

THE PARENTS WHO TOLD ME they worked all day, carted kids to practices on two different sports teams felt guilty about having no time for Church, so they enrolled their child in religious education. But they were angry with the religious coordinator and complained because classes interfered with their children's sports and their own lives.

MOST TEENAGERS' STORIES are competing for everything, what they look like, what they don't look like, what they are doing and what they can't do. The sad thing is nobody is telling them what's happening to them, and what to do about it, because their parents, teachers, and guardians are not teaching them what to do, like maybe buy the book, The Most Important Book You Will Ever Read by Jesus!

AN ELDERLY MAN, GEORGE, about 80 years old who I once visited spent his whole life making and living a very comfortable life style, traveling, golfing, and partying. Then his health deteriorated. He lost his wife, friends, could no longer do any of the things he had enjoyed his whole life. There he sat lonely, depressed, unable to do the things he used to. He was frightened of losing home. Where was he going to live? Who will take care of him? And how is he going to pay for it? With no children, he said, "I'm just waiting to die."

Seniors always ask me, "Father, I'm on a fixed income, I can't afford to do all those things I used to when I was young. So tell me what I am addicted to, because I'm still depressed and very lonely." If you are a senior, your stress, worry, loneliness comes from your addiction to the Kingdom of Man's way of thinking, that a comfortable, secure, and pleasurable lifestyle was and is the goal in life. You may believe that these activities that you're missing are the only way to be happy and fulfilled.

CHAPTER 11:
THE KINGDOM OF MAN BREAKING YOUR ADDICTIONS

Jesus gave us the answers to relieve stress, boredom and emptiness 2000 years ago. Again, many did not hear them, because they may have been "looking out the school window" at the Kingdom of Man.

BUT praise you, Jesus, because you did give the world these answers and showed us what to do about them and how to do it.

You might not like Jesus' answer.

<u>JESUS</u>:

> *If anyone would be my disciple, you must <u>DENY</u> yourself, pick up your cross, and follow me. (Mt. 16:24)*

You mean to tell me, Jesus, that in order to enter into the Kingdom of God, I have to <u>DENY</u> myself? What's wrong with wanting things that are not sinful and enjoying them, and what's wrong with doing things that are fun and bring me joy?

<u>JESUS</u>:

> *You cannot SERVE God and money. You will love the one and hate the other, cling to one, and despise the other.*

<u>JESUS' ANSWER IS</u>:

1. **SAYING "<u>NO</u>"** to the **KINGDOM OF MAN'S** way of thinking.

2. **PUTTING LIMITS & BOUNDARIES** on activities that I may have been addicted to and am in DENIAL about.

Jesus is not a "kill-joy." He did not say that you could not have possessions or do those things that you enjoy doing. He said that you cannot **SERVE** them and replace Him, His will for you, family, your church, and one another.

For us to enter into Jesus' way of thinking and living, He has to get us un-addicted first. Then we can refocus our attention on and follow Him. If you do not believe that, ask any addict in recovery and what they had to do to get liberated, set free, and enter their "new life."

After many years of knowing thousands of people in recovery, I have found them to be the most honest and trustworthy, because they were crucified by their addiction and are now raised from the dead through admittance of addiction and trusting in a greater power, the Lord.

LIMITS AND BOUNDARIES:

- Limiting the amount of time we spend doing the activities we want to do
- Limiting all we want to do all at the same time
- Boundaries on the number of other people whose activities we attend
- Limits and boundaries to grow in the ability to make a commitment and honor it, by sacrificing the desire that seems better or more fun

I have given this Kingdom of God and Kingdom of Man talk many times all over the country. I ask people to pray, ask the Lord for wisdom about what they may have been seduced by or addicted to in their lives, as it is different for each one of us. Then I tell them stories of what other people have done to be successful at setting themselves free, finding "The Kingdom of God."

Below are some of those ideas that have worked over a period of time.

LIMIT: Kids and Adults

- **LIMIT** TV, Cell/Telephone, Computer, iPad, iPod, electronic usage
- **LIMIT** Kids to the number of sports teams they are involved with, one in the fall/winter, one in the spring/summer, and one other activity (preferably at church or volunteering with family)
- **LIMIT** the amount of time for golf, hunting, fishing, shopping, personal entertainment
- **BOUNDARIES** on letting work and money define who and what your life is about so you can sustain a Kingdom of Man

lifestyle with all the toys and possessions

- ☐ **PUT BOUNDARIES** on the number of contacts and events to attend. With all the communication methods, cell phones, texting, email, and the invention of the automobile, we meet and know too many people. Take your time and think about it for a minute. Ask yourself how many calls, texts, emails, and Facebook contacts you receive or send a day. Because we are in touch with so many people, we are expected to immediately answer all of their calls, resulting in more stress from the time it takes. We have to go to all of their birthday celebrations, anniversaries, weddings, graduations, Baptisms, First Communions, retirement parties, etc. Don't forget gifts for all the above. Another frustrating experience is the guilt placed on us by people who expect us to go to all their activities and immediately return their calls and messages. If we don't, they feel ignored and rejected.
- ☐ **SAYING "NO"** TO UNNECESSARY SPENDING

The Kingdom of Man thinking has clouded our minds, no longer knowing the difference between what we want and what we need.

1. What I want arises from desires.

2. What I need arises out of necessities. This is food, clothing, shelter, and love. Anything more than these are really excesses. If you don't agree with this difference, I encourage you to volunteer at a soup kitchen, shelter, or visit a third world country.

STORYTIME:

A Woman from Seattle

I received a letter from a woman who attended a mission I gave about the Kingdom of Man and the Kingdom of God. She decided to put limits on her addiction to shopping for the latest fashions and clothing. I had to chuckle a little when she described her self-developed method that has given her success in knowing the difference between what she wants and what she needs.

When she goes shopping at a clothing store, she picks out what she really loves, tries it on, and enjoys looking at herself in the mirror of the dressing room. Then she puts her items in her cart and continues shopping. Here's the unique and wonderful way she says NO and puts LIMITS to her desires.

She continues shopping but continually looks at the sweater, dresses, and things in her cart, imagining that she already owns them and imagines all the places she can wear them. As she walks out of the store, she takes the items she can't imagine wearing from out of the cart and hangs them on the rack of items customers don't want to purchase.

Don't you love it? She also volunteers at her parish thrift store. Not bad from shopping for things she doesn't need at stores to managing a clothing store for those who really need them.

Men's Prayer Group

Every Saturday at 7am, when I am able I travel across the city to meet and pray with our men's group. These are men who have been baptized with the Holy Spirit and gather weekly as the early Christians did, to experience the Holy Spirit, to receive Wisdom, and discern the Lord's will for them, their marriages, and their family.

You can actually feel the Holy Spirit as we discuss the Scripture, helping one another to become better disciples of Jesus, husbands, and fathers. Here we learn how to discern what the Lord's Will is and also how to do it. The result is that our men's group is no longer a men's prayer group, but by having a shared experience of the Holy Spirit with each other, we have become "brothers" in every sense of the word. When any one of us is sick or going through hard times, we not only pray over the brother but make sure his family is taken care of, cutting the grass, shoveling snow, maintaining the house and making sure he has a ride to doctors and someone to go with him.

JESUS:

The way they will know that the Father sent me is by the way you love one another.

Personal Witness

I have met thousands of people from all over the country, giving retreats, missions, and talks. After several years of doing this and receiving hundreds of calls, emails, and texts from many of the thousands of people I met, I was overwhelmed and stressed by feeling obligated to answer them.

This started to affect my physical and mental health. Realizing that I had been seduced by the Kingdom of Man, I came home from giving five weeks of talks and having met another couple thousand people. I stopped at my sister's house and told her that the two worst inventions in the history of humanity are the telephone and automobiles. Seeing that I was really stressed out and meant it, she asked me, why.

"We know too many people who want to keep in touch and expect us to. When we don't, they get mad and lay a guilt trip on you."

Now I have to go to their weddings, birthdays, anniversaries, and buy all of them a gift, and less time for doing what I want to do.

That's when I took Jesus' words to heart and denied myself, setting limits and boundaries on my friends and acquaintances. Here's what I did and continue to do.

- ☐ I don't give out my phone number or email.
- ☐ When people say, "Father, let's keep in contact, I think we can become friends." My response is, **"I have a enough friends!"** They look at me in dismay, then I explain to them that I can't do that, because I have less and less time to be with my family but thanks for the invitation.
- ☐ I say "NO" to people's invitations to special events without lying or feeling guilty. Now this is something that will liberate all of you who are overwhelmed by this same problem.
- ☐ REMEMBER these four words. **Memorize them**, and you have my permission to use them to liberate yourself.

"I am not available."

(Repeat three times and memorize)

Next to the Word of God, I consider these words sacred and divinely inspired. Allow me to explain.

I received a call from North Carolina from a family I had met several years prior when hosting a retreat. Truly, they are a wonderful and loving family, and I had enjoyable memories of them. Little Jennifer, their daughter, had grown up and was getting married. She asked if I would perform the wedding ceremony on August 15. Mike, her dad, got on the phone and said he really wanted me to fly down, that he would wine and dine me, and after the wedding, we could play some tennis. Jennifer gets back on the phone and said that ever since she was a teenager she always said that she wanted Fr. Pompei to marry her and her future husband, because I was her favorite priest. Now there is pressure!

Because airplanes were invented, there should be no problem, right? The assumption of people and the Kingdom of Man mentality that has infected all of us is that I've been waiting here in my house for seven years, with nothing to do except wait for their call. Don't misunderstand me. It's wonderful that people befriend one another, and I'll be the first to say it's what keeps me going. My point here is that more and more people expect you to immediately drop everything and do what they are asking. Maybe I'm full of bologna about all this because I am a priest, and a cascade of people are constantly lining up to call and ask to do something and now.

Nevertheless, here is how I respond when I really don't want to do something. You have my permission to use these words.

"Jen, I am really sorry, but I'm not available on August 15. It would have been wonderful to be there. I'll put it on my calendar and will pray for the two of you on that day. Thanks for remembering and thinking about me. Give my best to you and your family."

Now your big question is, "What do I have to do on August 15 that is so important?"

NOTHING! *I don't have anything to do on August 15, because that's what I want to do on August 15 – NOTHING!*

Did I lie? No, I did not. I told the truth. I am **not available**, because I didn't want to fly down to North Carolina for four or five days and would rather do nothing, or something I wanted to do. Selfish? Guilty? No, because **I** made a choice to put limits and boundaries on my contacts and acquaintances, **so that I could focus more on the Lord, His Will, my family, and my church family** *(The Kingdom of God).*

<u>FREE AT LAST</u>

If you discipline yourself daily to sacrifice your desires for the sake of setting yourself free then you have taken your first step to enter into the great adventure Jesus is offering you in the **The Kingdom of God**. You might ask, what are some of the things you will experience and learn on your new life with the Lord? Well, you have been reading about them already, and there is so much more to come. The really Good News is that this is and will be the greatest adventure of your life, and the Best News is that it will never end.

POP QUIZ: *(Hint: The answer is one word.)*

The more you sacrifice, the more _____ you will have.

Answer in word jumble: MEIT _____

That's right, now you have **TIME**.

NOW YOU HAVE TIME, TIME, TIME.

TIME TO SAY

- ☐ Yes to talking and listening to Jesus and having a personal relationship with Him throughout your day.
- ☐ Yes to being quiet and learning to enjoy solitude. Be at peace when you are with yourself and God.
- ☐ Yes to spending more time with spouses, family and loved ones, listening, understanding, healing, supporting, enjoying, praying, and experiencing Jesus together.
- ☐ Yes to thinking differently about money, possessions and talents. They are blessings and gifts from God, not just for you, but to share with those who have few or none.
- ☐ Yes to focusing on your personal relationship with the Lord, church family, ministry and serving others, discerning God's Will, and doing it.

STORYTIME: IMPORTANCE OF SACRIFICING TO CREATE FAMILY

Dear Mom and Dad,

I am writing this letter to you from my retreat here at college. I remember how you wrote to me when I was on a high school retreat. I am sitting here in the chapel praying and thinking of how much Jesus and my faith mean to me and where my faith came from. It came from the both of you. I cannot tell you how grateful I am, but most of all, how much I love you.

Both of you have loved me unconditionally over the years. I know we have disagreed, and even argued about many things, but you always believed in me and were there for me. My relationship with both of you is different now. I feel so close to you. You have given me incredible gifts— my faith, my values, two loving brothers and a loving sister, and a family that is the constant strength in my life. My wish and prayer for you is a blessing.

I ask Jesus to give you great joy and happiness and fill you with his love. Thank you Mom and Dad for being the best parents, for believing in me, loving me, and for the family you have created.

With much love,

Michele

Michele is my adopted niece and has college-aged children of her own now. She is raising them the same way her parents raised her, with the Lord, faith, family, and the Church at the center of their lives and day.

I am a blessed man to have her parents as my friends, since we were in our early twenties. And after 45 years of friendship, they are no longer friends, but family. When Michele, her sister and brothers were little kids, they always called me "Uncle Fran," even though I was not their biological uncle.

I baptized and babysat for four years when they were babies, while their parents went to work in the evenings. It has always been a joy going to all their activities with much laughter and having them call "Uncle Fran" when they were in trouble with their parents. As a priest, it was always the deepest love I felt for them, and they for me, when we prayed with and over each other for healing or any problems we had. To have little children talk to Jesus for you and with you is just so incredible that it's difficult to describe.

What I have learned from it is when you experience God with another person, young or old, there is a BOND unlike any other relationship you have.

Furthermore, when they were kids, I found a lawyer. And the kids and I signed a legal contract for the nominal adoption of the title of "Uncle," "Nieces" and "Nephews." It was one of the best things I ever did. They have been a great source of joy and filled a lot of empty space in me as a celibate priest who wanted to marry and have my own children, but not permitted by the Church.

121

Here is a text message I received recently from Michele on Valentine's Day.

Uncle Fran, I just wanted to say Happy Valentine's Day to you! I love you and think and pray for you every day.

Much Love,

Your Niece - Michele

So, was it worth it for her parents to sacrifice what they wanted to do to enter the Kingdom of God? Was it worth it to deny themselves to live their marriage, raise their kids as a family, listening to, enjoying, praying with, and loving one another, involved with their church and ministry?

YOU BET IT WAS and continues to be. This is the joy, peace and love the Lord promised to give us. I hope and pray you will, if you have not already, experience these "God" moments in your life. You will if you choose to keep saying NO to living out of your desires, putting limits and boundaries on things, possessions, and all the activities you want or would rather do.

CHAPTER 12:
ENTERING THE KINGDOM OF GOD
GOD'S WAY OF THINKING AND LIVING

WHAT MIGHT GOD'S PLAN BE FOR YOU?

I have been shown different ways that people and parishes have entered into the Kingdom of God. When you, your family, or whoever you live with are searching for the Lord's plan for you, here are some possible things He may tell you that will draw your attention and spiritually "nudge" you. Remember, He will not force you, rather, invite you to choose freely.

MINISTRY:

- Go on service trips for a day, weekend, or week.
- Find people that may feel lonely in your neighborhood *(Catholic or not),* adopt them, bring them to church, include them as part of your family, invite them to Thanksgiving, Christmas dinner, and church events.
- Have a parish supper, but entrance fee are articles mentioned above.
- Join intercession prayer chains and groups.
- Visit hospitals and nursing homes.
- Volunteer at a soup kitchen or shelter.
- Volunteer for social justice groups, immigration, pro-life, and the environment.
- Volunteer for the bereavement ministry, serving a meal for the family and friends after the funeral mass of their loved one.
- Take care of the flowers and gardens around the Church.
- Go to daily Mass to be with your parish family to help one another in starting your day with the Lord.
- Teens, raise money for poor with Bottle and Can Drives.
- Teens and families, collect rare and much needed items for the poor and homeless, underwear, socks, feminine hygiene articles

COUPLES:

- Pray daily together; have daily walks; explore day and overnight trips; go to the gym; exercise; learn something

123

new; see theater shows and concerts; join prayer group together.

- ☐ Be Eucharistic ministers, grief ministers, outreach ministers, readers, and greeters in the parish. Go on weekend retreats. Sign up for Holy hours and Adoration together.
- ☐ Post notes on refrigerator, beds, mirrors, and car dashboards to express your love for one another. Give surprise gifts or a blindfold trip to a surprise event or place for your husband or wife.

FAMILIES:

- ☐ Hiking, camping, games.
- ☐ Gather in shared prayer, not just grace before meals.
- ☐ Do or learn something together as a family, *not just going to one member's event*, but a family event. This family day takes precedence over any other activity. Coaches are instructed that you are not available for any reason on that day.
- ☐ Go to the beach, picnics, camping, and museums.
- ☐ Go on a volunteer trip for a day or weekend.
- ☐ Volunteer at soup kitchen together.
- ☐ Volunteer the family for a Christian camp to help in disaster areas from hurricane, flooding, or earthquakes.
- ☐ Volunteer at an animal shelter or stable together.
- ☐ Prepare sandwiches and deliver them to people on the street.
- ☐ Visit a nursing home weekly or a couple times a month.
- ☐ Learn something new together as a family.
- ☐ Find unique activities, ice shows, the circus, parks. Watch a feel good movie together.
- ☐ Do chores together *(yard day- spring cleaning- community garden).*
- ☐ Rent a boat; go sliding; go fishing; go bowling; play a board game.

Be creative, and **do not let the world** tell you what to do, how to live to be a Christian family, married couple, child, teenager, young adult, or senior. **LET JESUS DO IT!**

Dream, add to the above suggestions, and do them. **Then you will enter into the Kingdom of God and experience the joy and love He promised.**

VERY IMPORTANT

Because you and I are still in school, do not expect all that you have learned, especially what to do and how to do it to be "perfect" or have immediate results. We will always be tempted and seduced by the Kingdom of Man until we graduate from this life. The goal is to examine your life periodically, asking the Lord to reveal how you may have slipped back into the Kingdom of Man mentality. Make sure you do not let Evil overwhelm you with guilt. Simply choose to make the necessary limits and boundaries to move the needle back to the Kingdom of God.

When you do this, the Good News is you will be choosing to focus off those things that have grabbed your attention too much and focus on the Lord, instead. I do believe that this is **TRUSTING** in the Lord, which if you remember, is your goal while here in school. So it's a win-win for you and a win-win for the Lord who loves you. And He puts a smile on His face, knowing you are paying attention and trying to do it.

The following is a "once in a while" ritual for you with your spouse and your whole family to examine your life and how much you may have or are being seduced back into the Kingdom of Man. Use it, and use it often. We live in a world where we are surrounded and out-numbered with Satan going around looking for someone to devour.

As the Prayer to St. Michael says,

Resist Him, steadfast in the faith.

SET FREE PRAYER

"DENY YOURSELF, PICK UP YOUR CROSS, AND FOLLOW ME."

LET'S PRAY:

Jesus, help me to be aware that you are right here with me.

(Pause 10 sec.)

Lord, it is good to be with you and my parish family!

Jesus, there's really a lot of stress in my life, too many things to do, and not enough time to do them. There are too many responsibilities and problems that are overwhelming. I worry about everything, and it even invades my sleep and affects my health.

Lord, you said, "Do not be afraid or let your hearts be troubled." I try to do this, but I cannot because my life has become so complicated. I have less and less time to think about you, the Church, and even my family.

Lord, have I replaced you with my desires... my desires for things that promise if I have them, use them, they will make me fulfill me and make me happy.

(Pause 10 sec.)

My desires are never fully satisfied, and then I am bored and unhappy. Like an addict, I need more and more things, bigger and better.

Lord, what are those things I am constantly thinking about and may have replaced you with?

(Pause 30 sec.)

Have I been addicted to this way of thinking and am unable to say No or put limits on the things that I think I cannot live without?

(Pause 15 sec.)

Lord, much of my stress also comes from having to do something all the time. When I am bored, lonely, and dissatisfied, these things are keeping me from you, my family, and my church.

So Jesus, what are those activities that I am doing more and more that I need to put limits on?

(Pause 15 sec.)

Think of activities you feel you can't give up or put limits on. They may be the ones you are addicted to.

Lord, you said that if I would be your disciple, I must **DENY** my very self, pick up my cross and follow you. I need to make some choices and deny myself, to free myself from thinking and living out of my desires so I can focus on You, what I was created for, and live according to Your will.

(Pause 30 sec.)

What service or ministry might Jesus be calling you and your family to?

Finally, Lord, I just want to be still, like you said, and be with you and my church family. I love you, Lord. Forgive me for placing other gods before you. *Close your eyes, take a deep breath, and just __BE__.*

(Pause 1 min.)

If you pray this with your spouse, family, or friends, then all stand. With your thumb, trace the sign of the cross on one another's forehead and say: "Lord, give us the grace to change."

Our Father... Amen!

<u>JESUS</u>:

I HAVE SOMETHING TO ASK OF YOU.

- *Will you set aside some time each day to be with Me?*
- *Will you turn off your cell phones, TVs, pray and have meals together, listening and enjoying your family and loved ones while doing more things together?*
- *Will you get more involved in your parish family and give some of your time to discern and do my will? Will you teach, serve, visit the sick, feed your poor brothers and sisters who need housing, clothing and a friend?*
- *Will you speak out and vote against injustices in your community and in the world? Poverty, Abortion, Immigration, the Environment, Terrorism, Oppression, and Corruption.*
- *Will you tell your stories of faith, containing the truths and values I have taught you? Whenever you do this, I will not only be with you, but will work through you.*
- *Will you love and forgive those who sin against you and leave judgment and their discipline up to me?*
- *So remember, seek first the Kingdom of God every day, so I can*

give you peace, not stress, but real Peace of Mind.

☐ *So talk this over with your family and those you live with. Put limits and boundaries to set yourself free, and then ask what My plan is for you and your family.*

Remember, I am counting on you, and believe in you. Most of all I love you, always have and always will.

CHAPTER 13:
YOUR DAILY ADVENTURE WITH JESUS

I hope you are beginning to experience the God who loves you and are "excited" about the road ahead. Even if you have been baptized by the Holy Spirit, what you are about to learn from Jesus may open up new gifts and new doors to open and follow.

When you have been baptized with the Holy Spirit and have passed over into the Kingdom of God, then your adventure with Jesus begins.

Remember how and when you experience the Holy Spirit is between you and the Lord, according to when He thinks you are ready.

Your adventure with the Lord is unique and different from everyone else's, because YOU are unique. Yet a relationship is a relationship and requires communication. For a personal relationship to deepen and grow, it must be a dialogue, and not a monologue. There must be talking and listening.

"When you pray, pray in the Spirit."

When people ask me how to deepen their faith and relationship with Jesus, I first ask them how they pray. Then I ask them what percentage of it is a monologue, and what percentage is a dialogue. After that I say "to deepen your faith and relationship with Jesus, you ought to learn how to listen to Him and how He communicates with you." In other words, Jesus actually reveals Himself to you with wisdom, direction and God's WILL for you each day, whatever you are doing and wherever you are.

Now I want to ask you, what is the percentage of your communication with God that is a dialogue? Or is it mostly a monologue with you doing all the talking? The question here that Jesus wants to answer and teach you is that YES, He can and does want you to trust Him with everything and anything that you want or need. But more importantly, He wants you to listen to Him and know that He is with you, forever.

THIS IS THE ADVENTURE, to grow in **awareness** by not only believing that Jesus is with you, but experience that He really is more and more.

A LITTLE EXERCISE:

Believing that Jesus is right there with you, tell Him from your heart and repeat **slowly three times**:

"Jesus, You are here. It's good to be with You."

I pray that you can see and imagine the smile you gave Him, because you simply chose to say the words from your heart and acknowledged Him and His love for you. I also hope you hear Him saying.

JESUS:

Thank you. I have long waited for You to call upon and invite me to be with you. I hope you will often be aware of Me with you, so we can walk together on the journey I have planned for your life. The safest place to be on your journey is with Me. I will never abandon you and hope you will never abandon Me.

HOW THE LORD COMMUNICATES

The question here is *Does the Lord really communicate and talk to you?* Rather than me trying to explain the answer to you, I have included the **various ways** that others and myself have a dialogue relationship with Jesus below.

THROUGH A SITUATION: A young man named Tim, senior in college, decided to take an alternative Spring Break and volunteered for a week at St. Francis Inn Soup Kitchen in Philadelphia. His plan was to get his master's degree in engineering, but after living and working with the poor, feeding them, waiting on and befriending them, He experienced the Holy Spirit and Jesus.

In his own words, "I actually felt Jesus in the people when I spent time talking to them." Does the Lord communicate and reveal His Will to us? You bet He does. How do I know that? Tim postponed his grad school plans and volunteered two more years at the soup kitchen.

SCRIPTURE: When my sister faced cancer and surgery, she was over come by fear and worry. She initially asked the Lord for a miracle. When her fear intensified and she became more anxious, she opened her Bible and read words of Jesus that jumped off the page as if Jesus was right there saying them to her personally.

"While you are in the world you will suffer, but don't be afraid, for I am with you. Trust in God and Trust in me."

She prayed for healing but prayed for the grace to Trust in Jesus and let go of her fear by not dwelling on her cancer and surgery. Instead she focused on the Lord with her and on doing things she would ordinarily do to keep her attention from centering on her cancer. It was not magic, because that's not how Trust works.

She was still tempted and attacked by fear, but kept choosing to tell Jesus she trusted Him, and she let go. Little by little, the grace she asked for was given to her, because she experienced this peace and less and less fear or worry.

The day of her surgery, two of her friends and myself were waiting for the doctors to call her down. We prayed with her and again she simply said, "I trust in you, Jesus. Your Will be done." When we finished, my sister who has a great wit, made us laugh with funny one-liners about her surgery. All of us, my sister included, felt absolutely no fear or worry.

When the doctor and nurse walked in, we were having a full belly laugh. Later the doctor told my sister that in all his years doing surgery, he never experienced someone so unafraid and overcome with laughter as they wheeled her into surgery.

My sister told him that Jesus told her to trust Him, and she did. Does Jesus communicate and reveal his will for us through His words? You bet He does, definitely, according to my sister.

DIRECT FROM THE LORD: My brother, now a retired diocesan priest, while on a long retreat as a young priest received two direct words from the Lord, calling him to a prophetic preaching ministry. He made the leap of faith and trusted in the Lord, and his life and ministry changed radically.

Since that time he has preached and given the Lord's Word and prophecies to many thousands of people all over the United States and Europe. He has also prophesied to the institutional church, parishes, and individuals. Like many prophets, he was mocked, belittled, and considered a "persona non grata" (someone unwanted or appreciated in a setting). However, by trusting in the Lord and living by the guidance of the Holy Spirit, Jesus has been able to forgive, heal, guide, and give hope to many more people than he would have if my brother stayed in parish ministry.

Does Jesus reveal His Will and Plan for our lives directly? Ask my brother!

For to one is given by the Spirit the <u>Word of Wisdom</u>, to another the <u>Word of Knowledge</u> by the same Spirit. (1 Cor. 12:8)

<u>CHURCH TEACHINGS</u>: All Christian religions believe in the forgiveness of our sins, because of Jesus shedding His blood on the cross with the saving words, "Father, forgive them for they know not what they do."

Phil is a man I visited in a maximum-security prison who had attempted suicide a couple times for his horrific crimes, feeling nothing left to live for. He was an atheist his whole life and lived according to his own desires and beliefs. I told him there was another way besides suicide, and that I knew how to lead him there, without preaching to him or trying to proselytize him.

In short, I told him that the God who created Him would not only forgive him, but He unconditionally loved Him before he sinned, while he was sinning, and after he sinned.

I left him with a decision to make. *If you hate your life, would you be willing to give it to Jesus and ask for His forgiveness?* He said Yes the following week, and we prayed together. When he was praying and surrendering his life to Jesus, he burst into hysterical sobbing, and all of his self-hatred poured out.

Then he looked up at me, half-dazed and said, "Jesus is really here, isn't He?"

I said, "And He really loves you."

The Christian church teaches that Jesus forgives our sins. Ask Phil if he not only believes this but experienced it.

Phil is no longer an atheist.

THROUGH OTHERS: *(Sometimes the most unlikely)*

Yes, the Lord can and does answer our prayers through other people, and sometimes by those we least expect. They can even be unaware that they are the answer to your prayer.

The Lord can bring more good out of this way of answering your prayers, because you just may be the answer to theirs. The Lord doesn't force us but sets up the connection of people and hopes we are open to giving to one another not only answers but also Peace of Mind, healing, and even forgiveness.

Let me explain.

PERSONAL STORY:

When I was at a soup kitchen in Philadelphia where we fed 300 people a day, twice a day, we friars lived across the street from the kitchen in a row house in what the TV program Nightline reported was one of worst neighborhoods in the United States.

There were always five to 10 people sleeping on cardboard on the sidewalk in front of our door and at the soup kitchen. I couldn't sleep one night, decided to go outside to the kitchen to get some milk.

For two or three weeks, I was going through the motions, but inside I was "burnt out," getting conned, threatened, and constantly ripped off. I started becoming cynical and questioned what I was doing with my life. I sure did not feel like a Franciscan priest or Brother to the people.

When I walked out of the friary onto a piece of cardboard, there he was, "Cincinnati", as he wanted to be called. He was one of the worst con men at the kitchen, and I was his worst confronter. We were like oil and water.

So he immediately woke up as I opened the door, got up on his knees and told me he had to go to the bathroom and that he was hungry. I wasn't in the mood for his lies and con job, so my first response was *No*.

Then he kept demanding and begging as usual. So, reluctantly, he followed me to the soup kitchen. I opened the door of the bathroom and waited for him to finish. As he left, he saw two donuts left over from the day before and asked to take them, once again in his demanding voice. I simply said *Take them*. All I wanted to do was get a glass of milk.

When I finished and started walking back to the friary, I remember thinking *Not a great start of the day again, Lord. I have no idea where you are and what's happening to me.*

When I got to the friary door, there was Cincinnati waiting for me. What did he want now? Then he put his hand on my shoulder, looked at me with a look that I had never seen before, touched my cheek, and with a heartfelt voice said, *"Brother Francis, you are a **real** Brother."* After three weeks of self pity, the Lord spoke and reminded me what I was, that He had been with me and loved me." That's the adventure of the Lord. His answer to my prayer came through a poor street person named Cincinnati.

After that morning, we became friends, but he still conned me. However, it was a lot less this time. And he did, we'd both laugh.

So keep your spiritual eyes and ears open for the answers to your prayers, because Jesus is full of surprises. You can end up with more than you ask for.

<u>**CONNECTING DOTS**</u>: Did you ever meet someone, a complete stranger, and circumstances led you to help them? Or they helped you in a deep way that really answered both of your prayers? Afterwards, as you reflected on it you felt that it was no coincidence, rather it had been planned without forcing you to recognize, help, guide, or even heal one another.

When I said that entering the Kingdom of God is the great adventure the Lord offers us every day by discovering His plan for us and not just ours for Him—I call it Connecting the Dots. Do you remember that coloring book where we didn't see the whole picture until we looked for and found the next dot to connect them all? For me, this has been and continues to be the most exciting way to do God's Will.

This is how it works for me. I have my list of things I want or have to do each day, but I am open and look for God's dots that start connecting. Then the more I connect them, the more I know it's not a coincidence, but Him revealing His Will to me for the person or the situation I'm in.

The moment I "get it" and see the whole picture, I can sense the Lord with me, offering His answer to a prayer. Many times, He answers mine through a person or situation. When it's over, there is the realization that this was a God moment and experience, because we connected the dots.

GOD'S ANSWER- THE 1%

The Lord taught me this when I was in my early twenties as I decided that He was calling me to priesthood. I call it the 1% prayer. Up until then I asked God to help me with serious decisions by telling me what I should do and what His Will was.

However, most of the time I didn't feel as if God was listening and certainly not telling me what I should do. I even said in my prayer that I was "thick and dumb" and needed His answer to be obvious and crystal clear. That didn't even work.

Then I received some great spiritual direction. A holy person told me that Jesus is always going to respect my freedom to choose, because He knows that is how we will learn how to trust. Then he gave me a formula when asking for God's input in decision-making. Bingo, the 1% discernment method. Before this, I always expected the Lord to give me the answer with 100% certitude and make it completely obvious.

Well, here it is. I have made every major decision in life, using the 1% method, and the Lord has taught me that it works.

If you have a choice to make between two paths to take and are attached to both at 50% each, unable to make a decision, then stop asking the Lord for 100% certitude. Just ask Him for 1%, be patient and wait. Keep asking, and keep your spiritual ears and eyes open. But let go of it.

When you are ready, and many times when you least expect it, He will give you the 1%. The best part is that you will know that it is not from you, but Him. Now, here is better news, because it's only 1%, you can still have 49% leaning toward or convinced of the other way. Because you are still in school, this is how the Lord gives you the opportunity to TRUST in Him by trusting in the 1%.

This is how I had to break off the relationship with a beautiful young woman that I was pursuing and enter the seminary. I can tell you it was very difficult, but that was my choice... to Trust in the Lord. It was an extremely lonely year with many doubts, but by the end of the year, I was at 55% and decided to keep trusting the now 5%.

In the end, I became a deacon at about 80% and a priest at around 90%. It's been that way for my whole priesthood, but now that I am an old friar, it's 99%. Yet 1% if me always wonders what my life would have been like if I chose the other path. And because I'm still in school, that's OK.

So does the Lord help us with our decisions, reveal His plan and Will to us? The co-author of this book, me, says **ABSOLUTELY!**

<u>YOU</u>: Because God created you so wonderfully unique, and the relationship you have with the Lord is between you and Him, He may have given you a personalized way to reveal Himself and His will for you. So all the above that I have learned from people's experience, as well as my own, you can add to yours. That should keep you busy walking with the Lord!

<u>KNOWING THE DIFFERENCE</u>: YOUR WILL AND THE LORD'S

The last thing I want to share with you, regarding discernment of the Lord's Will, is the importance of knowing the difference between God's Will *(what He wants us to do)* and YOUR will for Him and the Church.

I invite all believers, especially those in positions of leadership ministry, whether you are the pastor, rabbi, imam, or director of a ministry in your community, to listen carefully to the following.

<u>**JESUS**</u>: *I have come to do the Will of my Father. Not my will, Father, but Yours. ...Thy Kingdom come, **THY WILL** be done.*

Jesus teaches us to discern God's Will *(what He wants us to do, and not what we think He wants.)* If you don't learn this and spend most of your time doing everything for everybody, because you think this is what you are supposed to do for the Lord, the Church, and His people, **you're heading for disaster**. This way of thinking is a recipe for frustration and feeling overwhelmed, not to mention the effects on your physical and mental health. You might also add your spiritual health to the mix.

The answer is to ask the Holy Spirit for the **Gift of Discernment** to know the difference between the two.

Since you now know the ways Jesus reveals His Will to us - learning the difference will help you to say **No**, that you are **Not available**, or **refer** them to someone who would be able to help them, and do it without guilt. It will also help you to say **Yes** to those you sense the Lord wants you to help and doing what He wants you to do.

EXERCISE: Practice this by periodically doing a spot check on your ministry and volunteering, to see if you are moving toward what the Lord is asking or what other people are asking of you.

POINT of CONTEXT: With the media, cell phones, Internet, social media, communication is off the charts. How does this translate into ministry? We know too many people. Then when we are invited to many places, our **good will** kicks in, and if we say *No,* we feel guilty. Without our knowing it, we are pushed toward the Kingdom of Man, because we have less and less time with the Lord and our families.

"During the night, Jesus went to the other side of the lake to a secluded place." (Mk. 1:35)

To remember the different ways Jesus reveals His Will to us, and the difference between His Will and ours, keep the following story in your heart and mind.

STORYTIME:

An elderly widowed mother raised her three children in a three-room row house of the ghetto. When her children grew up, they left home and became multi-millionaires. Living in different parts of the country, they called each other and discussed the gifts they were able to give their elderly mother for her birthday.

- **Steve** said, "I built a big mansion for Mom with 30 rooms. It cost one million dollars. Now Mom can get out of that ghetto dump."
- **Lisa** said, "You know how Mom never goes out, so I sent her a Rolls Royce car with a driver 24/7. Now she can go where ever she wants and whenever she pleases."
- **Christopher** said, "I've got you both beat. You know how Mom enjoys reading the Bible, but now she can't see very well? I sent her a parrot that can recite the entire Bible. It took 20 monks from Tibet 10 years to teach this parrot. I had to pledge 50 thousand dollars a year for 10 years, but it was worth it. All Mom has to do is say the chapter and verse, and the parrot will recite it.

So Mom sent out her letters of thanks.

- **"Steve,"** she wrote to her first son. "I've lived in three rooms my whole life. The house you built is too big. I live in only one room, but I have to clean the whole house."
- **"Lisa,** I'm too old to travel. I stay home all the time, so I never use the car. And the driver is rude!"
- **"Christopher,"** she wrote to her third son, **"You were the only one who knew what your mother really wanted...**

That chicken was delicious   Love, Mom

I know; silly anecdote. But it will remind you to ask for the **gift of discernment** to know the difference of doing the Lord's will and yours for him. If you don't, you will burn out, be discouraged, frustrated, cynical, and be tempted to quit and leave, whether it's church, faith, service, etc. *(Exactly what Satan and Evil wants you to do)*

CONCLUSION:

- The Lord can and wants to communicate with you.
- The relationship He wants with you is a dialogue, not a monologue.
- There are many ways He can communicate with you and

tailored just for you.

- The Holy Spirit can give you the gift of discernment to determine what's from you, the world, and what is from the Lord.
- The Lord has a plan and His Will for you every day, which is the great adventure He offers all of us.
- The Lord will not interfere with your freedom. It's up to you to choose to know and experience Him and the Holy Spirit.
- It all begins when you ask, seek, and knock for the Baptism of the Holy Spirit. When you are ready, according to Jesus, YOU WILL.
- Keep your spiritual eyes and ears open for the different ways He will communicate and speak to you personally.

CHAPTER 14:
FINAL EXAMS AND GRADUATION (Physical Death)
WHAT TO DO & HOW TO DO IT!

When your body enters into the process of dying, school is finally almost over. The suffering you or a loved one is enduring are final exams, and from what you have learned, it is the last time to TRUST instead of succumbing to the negative thoughts, half-truths, and lies of Evil that are violently attacking and overwhelming you. It is Satan's one last chance to steal your Spirit, light, and soul by tempting you to doubt God or despair and forsake Him.

Remembering what you learned about Satan, Evil, and how it works by putting thoughts and images in your mind, it will now be a final test of how much you have grown and practiced the steps to trust in the Lord. If you have not spent your life working on your diploma of Trust that God sent you here to learn, then this will determine the degree that you will let fear, terror, panic, depression, doubt, and despair control your mind, emotions, and feelings.

Evil will convince you, as it has most people, that death is the end of you and your existence. It is here that you need to remember what Jesus taught you about Suffering and Death. They are not the real enemy when your physical body is ending. It is your FEAR of them. **THAT IS WHAT JESUS ACCOMPLISHED ON THE CROSS.**

He refused to succumb to the temptation of Fear, the end of His life, and feelings of being abandoned by GOD *(His Father)*. With His last words, He **TRUSTED** by choosing to focus off the evil thoughts and lies in His mind. He focused His attention on His Father in Heaven *as we all did when we were children and frightened and immediately focused off the pain and called for Mommy.* **Remember?**

JESUS:

I was tempted by the thoughts and images of suffering that I would experience and succumbed to Satan's power of Fear.

"Father, let this cup of suffering pass me by."

140

My fear turned into terror, and Satan threw me into agony and despair, so I cried out...

"Father, I beg you, let this cup of suffering pass me by..."

*Then I focused off the thoughts and images of Suffering and Death that I would experience the next day and even though Satan and Fear were still attacking Me, **I chose** to pray to My Father and be given the Strength and love to Trust Him anyway.*

"Father, if this cup will not pass, and I must drink of it, then let it be done according to your will and not mine."

Finally, I found some peace in the midst of my suffering. The most important thing is that it was my Father's and my unconditional love for you that drove me to do it.

These attacks and temptations do not end once we Trust. They can and will continue to attack many times more intensely. That is why when you are in the "waiting rooms of life" in your doctor's office or waiting for the condition of your loved one to change for the better, even after you pray, you are still attacked, RIGHT?

However, the more you do the Steps to TRUST, and they become more natural to you, the easier it gets to train your mind to **not** download the evil thoughts, let go of them, and give them to the Lord. As you learned in the chapter on suffering, you may have to do this hundreds of times in the waiting rooms of life and continue to do it for the rest of your life until you graduate from school and leave your body.

Do **not** give up and **do** not surrender. When tempted, **ATTACK**, **ATTACK**, and then **ATTACK** some more. Remember again what St. Paul said.

Our battle is not against flesh and blood, but the evil principalities, powers, and rulers of the Kingdom of Darkness in the Heavens. (Eph. 6:12)

What Jesus is teaching us is that **Trusting** is the constant and the central action of our faith in Him and the Father. The Truth is that there is a WAR going on in our bodies and in our Mind. As I said before, it is a battle for our very soul, and the good news is that the Kingdom of God is now here. The Son of God, Jesus, our Lord and Savior, has won and given us the strength to endure our suffering, and He has given us the power and WILL to fight and resist Fear and Evil, as He did His.

A SUMMARY TEACHING:

Jesus has taught and told you what to do and shown you how to do it, so it is up to you to choose to not only believe it as the Truth and God's Will, but **DO IT!**

Do not let fear keep you on the bleachers as in the Parable of the "High Wire Walker" in Chapter 2. Jesus is in the wheelbarrow when you TRUST, and it is up to you to take action and get in.

JESUS CONQUERS OUR FEAR OF DEATH, AT THE END OF OUR EARTHLY LIFE

Jesus conquers Death by the RESSURECTION, His Transformation and the re-creation of His human body that was subject to Evil's Suffering and Death. What Jesus did by His Resurrection was form a renewed body, a perfect and divine physical body—**YOURS, YOUR FUTURE**, and **NOT** Death.

JESUS:

As I said to Martha, at the death of her brother and my close friend, Lazarus, I say to you now and ask you to listen very carefully.

I am the Resurrection and Life itself, if you believe and trust in me. When your physical body dies, I will raise you, your Spirit, Mind and Soul to live forever with Me and with a re-created, perfect spiritual and physical body.

*My question to Martha as it is and will continue to be for you, especially when you are suffering and your earthly body is dying, is **DO YOU BELIEVE?***

NEUROSURGEON Dr. Eben Alexander

"I have spent decades, as a neurosurgeon and scientist, at some of the most prestigious medical institutions, but because of my coma and NEAR death experience, I now know beyond a doubt that our consciousness lives on after our physical brains and bodies die. We are actually set free to a higher level of knowing, and the Universe is defined by an Unconditional Love for us. And that Unconditional Love is God."

Dr. Eben Alexander is a Harvard-trained neuro and brain surgeon who was an agnostic, but not anymore. He had a near-death experience of God and Heaven. For more of his incredible story, his book is entitled Proof of Heaven. You can also find a wonderful convincing interview on YouTube.

I highly recommend reading his story as he details his experience, not just of God and Heaven, but something that happened to him there that convinced him, without a doubt, that this all took place outside of his brain and physical body.

I included this story, because I not only believe it is true, but it represents that Science, Psychology, and credible people with more and more near-death have similar experiences.

Recommendation: One of my favorite books I give to people who are getting ready for graduation is Embraced by the Light by Betty Eadie. From the hundreds of books I have read about people going to Heaven, I believe that Eadie had the most extensive experience of what Heaven is like and will look like, and the many levels. She also discusses how we travel and communicate with creatures and creations. She vividly describes who and what our lives in Heaven were like before we chose to come here on earth, why we chose to come, God's plan for us, and so much more.

People preparing to graduate who read Embraced by the Light have all said that it not only answered many of their questions about death, but delivered them from their fear of the unknown and gave them a new hope to leave their bodies.

Personally, I love the book and often go back to read it again and again.

EXTREMELY IMPORTANT DRILL:

If you are an "old timer" like me, do you remember having to write on the blackboard 100 times *I will not talk in class?*

Well, repeat the following at least three times before you continue and repeat whenever anybody brings up death and dying. Memorize and use it as the absolute truth whenever attacked by Satan's lies. When you do, you will experience the power and authority of Jesus. That's why He taught us how to pray, "...deliver us from EVIL."

He doesn't want you to just to say the words but do it. So, get to it and memorize this Truth, let it guard you and deliver you from your fears and worries.

Alleluia, Jesus!!!

START:

- ☐ **DEATH IS GRADUATION & COMMENCEMENT IS ETERNAL LIFE.**
- ☐ **DEATH IS GRADUATION & COMMENCEMENT IS ETERNAL LIFE.**
- ☐ **DEATH IS GRADUATION & COMMENCEMENT IS ETERNAL LIFE.**
  (Repeat three times)

Do you want to help people who are losing or have lost a loved one? Then make it a point to never use the words DEATH or DYING. Instead, tell the whole world what you have learned from Jesus in this book. You can use my words to respond to people when they say the following

THEM:	"My mother is dying!"
ME:	**"Oh, they're getting ready to "graduate."**

THEM:	"My mother died."
ME:	"Oh, they graduated. I'm awfully sorry. I'll pray the Lord will heal you "missing them" with the knowledge that you will see them again when you graduate."

I developed mine by just putting into words what the Lord taught me about dying, death, and graduation. By making these your new responses, trust me, you will not only replace Satan's lie but heal and give the person hope that their loved one is not dead, but only their body is. And they will see them again.

When you do, you will feel the Holy Spirit speaking through you, offering Jesus' healing and love for the person.

ST. PAUL & the OLD TESTAMENT:

- ☐ *"Our citizenship is in Heaven." (Phil. 3:20)*
- ☐ *"Before I knit you in your mother's womb, I knew you." (Jer. 1:5)*
- ☐ *"Therefore we do not lose heart, but though our outer body is decaying, our inner spirit is being renewed day by day. For our suffering and affliction is TEMPORARY (school) and producing for us an eternal HOME (graduation-new life) and a glory far beyond all comparison." (2 Cor. 4:16)*
- ☐ *"Behold! I tell you a mystery. We shall not all sleep, but we shall all be changed in a moment, in the twinkling of an eye at the last trumpet. The trumpet will sound, and the dead will be raised imperishable, and we shall be changed." (1 Cor. 15:51-53)*

Having learned all that you have so far, I want to ground it in reality through actual human experience.

SUMMARY OF JESUS' TEACHINGS

REGARDING DEATH, TRUTH TO SET YOU FREE

LIES	THE TRUTH
☐ Death is the end of my life. ☐ My mother, father, husband, child is dead. I will never see them again. I will never be able to live without them. ☐ Why did God take them? The loneliness is unbearable.	☐ Only my physical body and brain die. I will live forever. ☐ My loved ones are alive, only their physical bodies have ended. They have graduated and have gone home. ☐ I will see them again, when I graduate and for all eternity.

GRADUATION FROM SCHOOL

"LETTING GO"

Dying is simply letting go, which you have done from the beginning and throughout your whole life.

- ☐ Leaving Heaven to be conceived here
- ☐ Leaving the swaddling comfort of your mother's womb
- ☐ Leaving for kindergarten and school, family, home, geography, friends, experiences, careers, activities that we enjoyed doing
- ☐ Letting go of your youth, parents, grandparents, spouses, siblings, health, and eventually your physical body

What makes letting go easier is TRUSTING in the Lord. There is that VERB again that by now, hopefully, Jesus has drilled in your mind and soul. It is what to do throughout your body's dying process. So my Uncle Tony was right when he told me he wasn't afraid of dying, and he was at peace, because he **Trusted** in the Lord his whole life." *Francis, I only have to **Trust** Him one more time."*

Now that's the great reward of paying attention while we are here in school and listening to our Teacher, Jesus. **ALLELUIA!**

A PLAN FOR THE DEATH OF YOUR BODY

146

This is probably one of, if not, the best gifts from Jesus to you—a Real Plan for your own death. WHAT? I am not kidding—a Real Plan to deliver you from the Fear of YOUR own Death. It is a step-by-step plan by Jesus Himself. Jesus not only has taught us about Suffering and Death, what to do about them, but also showed us how to do it.

He is going to teach you about your own death, what thoughts you need to stop downloading that the world has burned into your mind. Then download His truth and dwell on them for the rest of your life and even on graduation day.

<u>JESUS</u>:
First, I want you to replace your thoughts and the images of your own death that are lies with the TRUTH and ME.

YOU PICTURE DEATH AS COMING TO DESTROY YOU
Picture instead Me, taking you to your real home in Heaven, where I created you.

YOU THINK OF DEATH AS YOUR LIFE ENDING
The Truth is that your new life is just beginning.

YOU THINK OF YOUR GOING AS A LOSS
Think instead of what you will find— freedom from Fear, Suffering, Death, and Eternal Life, which no human words can describe.

YOU THINK OF PARTING FROM YOUR FAMILY
Think rather that you will meet God who has always unconditionally loved you. Think about all the people who loved you, who are already here with Me.

YOU THINK OF DEATH AS LEAVING
Think of yourself as arriving in Heaven, your real home, and eternal life forever.

SO, WHEN THE VOICE OF DEATH WHISPERS TO YOU
You are dying and your life is ending, hear My voice saying that you are graduating from your body and coming home with Me forever.

I want you to read these over and over, especially when Satan, dragging you down with fear, anger, doubt, and despair, attacks your mind. Remember to read them to your loved ones, too, and anyone who is ready to graduate.

It will not only deliver them from their fear, but encourage them to Trust, walk across the stage, get their diploma, leave the school building, commence and begin their new eternal life with Me and their loved ones who are already there waiting.

WHAT TO DO, THINK, AND PRAY WHEN THE MOMENT OF YOUR BODY'S DEATH BEGINS

Do you remember having a graduation rehearsal the night before the big day, so you would know exactly what to do the next day? Well, here are the rehearsal details of what to do, what to pray, and how to think when your body is dying.

As your senses quit functioning, things will start to dim. You may feel like you are in darkness, like many who have had near death experiences feel they are in a tunnel.

THE PLAN:

- Don't be afraid and give in to lies, doubt and despair.
- Keep using your **WILL** to let go of your physical senses, and not try to make them function or be afraid they are not working.
- You will still be very aware of your Self, Consciousness, Mind, and Will. Using your WILL, choose to let go of your family, friends, and earthly life. This will be very difficult, but keep doing it, and keep reminding yourself what Jesus taught you. You will see them again when they pass over and graduate.
- Then focus off your body dying and **look for Jesus and your loved ones who have already graduated.**
- Keep talking to them and asking them to come for you. No matter how intense your feelings of fear, doubt, and despair may be, use your **WILL** and keep choosing to look for Jesus and your loved ones until they come. Do so by repeating the words of Jesus on the cross when His body was dying.

"Into your hands, Lord, I commend my spirit."

- When you sense, see, or hear Jesus and your loved ones, do whatever they tell you to do and go wherever they tell you to go.
- Don't be tempted to listen or go with anyone else, no matter how good it feels.
- Don't look back.

148

*Even if your physical body and brain is in a coma, your Consciousness, Mind, and Soul will still be in tact for you to follow the PLAN, cross over, and GRADUATE.

HALLELUJAH!

Your Graduation Rehearsal is over. Now you know what to do and how to do it.

If you have listened to everything Jesus taught you, He is now calling you, not only to do it, but also to witness and preach the good news to all who you meet.

As long as you are in your body, remember you are still in school. Keep paying attention and walk with the Lord every day. Use the Holy Spirit as your guide and strength to grow in Unconditional Love, Forgiveness, and Generosity.

CHAPTER 15:
GOD'S WISDOM FOR LIFE

Your spiritual and moral compass according to Jesus & the Word of God

JESUS said, *Heaven and Earth will pass away, but my Words will never pass away.* (Mt. 24:35)

Here is the Word of God that will remind you of what He has taught you and give you the power and authority of speaking the Truth to yourself and to a world that has abandoned it.

WHO IS JESUS?

JESUS SAID, "I AM THE WAY, THE TRUTH AND THE LIFE."

☐ A personal relationship with Jesus is what will lead YOU to your ultimate fulfillment and eternal home.

JESUS SAID, "I AM THE LIGHT OF THE WORLD."

☐ Jesus gives YOU your real meaning, and reveals to YOU who and what YOU are.

JESUS SAID, "I AM THE GOOD SHEPHERD. THE GOOD SHEPHERD LAYS DOWN HIS LIFE FOR HIS SHEEP."

☐ Jesus' love is willing to die for YOU.

JESUS SAID, "I AM THE BREAD OF LIFE. HE WHO COMES TO ME SHALL NEVER BE HUNGRY."

☐ Like food, Jesus' love will keep YOU healthy.

JESUS SAID, "I AM THE DOOR. IF ANYONE ENTERS BY ME, HE WILL BE SAVED."

☐ A relationship with Jesus is the way to HAPPINESS.

JESUS SAID, "I AM AMONG YOU AS ONE WHO SERVES. "

☐ Jesus wants YOU to treat Him as a "Friend" not as a God who dominates. Jesus wants YOU to serve and treat others in the same way, as sisters and brothers.

JESUS SAID, "I AM THE TRUE VINE, AND YOU ARE THE BRANCHES."

☐ YOU need to pray (talk with Jesus) regularly.

JESUS SAID, "I AM THE RESURRECTION AND THE LIFE. HE WHO BELIEVES IN ME, EVEN IF HE DIES, SHALL LIVE."

☐ There is an after-life, eternal life forever with Jesus. And a personal relationship with Jesus is the way YOU get there. As St. Paul describes it, "We can't even begin to imagine how wonderful it will be."

JESUS SAID, "I AM IN THE FATHER, AND THE FATHER IS IN ME."

☐ Jesus is "GOD." Jesus is **YOUR** God. Jesus is **YOUR** Lord. Jesus is **OUR** Lord.

JESUS SAID, "I AM WHO AM."

☐ Jesus is "Life" and "Existence" itself.

LOVE

"GOD IS LOVE AND ANYONE WHO LOVES, KNOWS GOD, FOR GOD IS IN THEM."

☐ You can know God when YOU give of yourself to others.

"GOD SHOWS HIS LOVE FOR US BY JESUS DYING FOR US WHEN WE WERE SINNERS."

☐ Not many people would die for YOU. But Jesus did.

"GOD SO LOVED THE WORLD THAT HE GAVE HIS ONLY SON, THAT WHOEVER BELIEVES IN HIM MIGHT BE SAVED AND HAVE ETERNAL LIFE."

- ☐ "Saved" YOU from death and meaninglessness.

"LOVE IS PATIENT, KIND, AND DOES NOT REJOICE IN WRONGDOING, BUT REJOICES IN THE TRUTH. LOVE ENDURES ALL THINGS."

- ☐ It's obvious.

"GREATER LOVE HAS NO MAN THAN TO LAY DOWN HIS LIFE FOR HIS FRIENDS."

- ☐ Jesus laid down his life for YOU. YOU need to do the same for others.

"YOU SHALL LOVE THE LORD WITH ALL YOUR HEART, SOUL, AND MIND AND YOUR NEIGHBOR AS YOURSELF."

- ☐ God should be the center of YOUR attention and life.

"THE WAY PEOPLE WILL KNOW YOU ARE MY DISCIPLE IS BY THE WAY YOU LOVE ONE ANOTHER."

- ☐ Live the Gospel. Don't just talk about it.

"LOVE YOUR ENEMIES, DO GOOD TO THOSE WHO HATE YOU. IF YOU LOVE ONLY THOSE WHO LOVE YOU, WHAT CREDIT IS THERE IN THAT? EVEN SINNERS LOVE ONE ANOTHER. I SAY LOVE YOUR ENEMIES."

- ☐ Jesus did it and wants YOU to do the same.

"LOVE CONSISTS OF THIS, NOT THAT WE LOVE GOD, BUT RATHER THAT HE LOVED US FIRST."

- ☐ YOU can't know or give what you have never experienced.

BEATITUDES
(God's promises and the Gospel Life)

"BLESSED ARE THE POOR FOR THE KINGDOM OF GOD IS THEIRS."

- The poor and broken have no masks to hide behind. In their powerlessness, they need and must trust in God to provide. Jesus calls and invites YOU to be poor in spirit, and in brokenness, trust in HIM.

"BLESSED ARE THEY WHO MOURN, FOR THEY WILL BE COMFORTED."

Jesus suffers with YOU and offers YOU His presence, strength, and hope.

"BLESSED ARE THE MEEK, THEY WILL INHERIT THE LAND."

When YOU are meek, YOU will "respect" and won't abuse the Earth and others.

"BLESSED ARE THEY WHO HUNGER AND THIRST FOR HOLINESS, THEY WILL HAVE THEIR FILL."

- If YOU want to grow and deepen your relationship with Jesus, YOU can.

"BLESSED ARE THE MERCIFUL, FOR THEY WILL RECEIVE MERCY."

- Jesus forgives YOU and wants you to forgive others the same way.

"BLESSED ARE THE PURE OF HEART, FOR THEY SHALL SEE GOD."

- Lord, when YOU don't judge and remain innocent, YOU will see GOD clearly.

"BLESSED ARE THE PEACEMAKERS, FOR THEY WILL BE CALLED CHILDREN OF GOD."

- ☐ When YOU are an instrument to settle arguments, YOU create and become "family."

"BLESSED ARE THEY WHO ARE PERSECUTED FOR THE SAKE OF RIGHTEOUSNESS, FOR THE KINGDOM OF HEAVEN WILL BE THEIRS."

- ☐ Doing what's right doesn't always feel good in the present, but will ultimately lead YOU to the Lord and the good that YOU seek.

"BLESSED ARE YOU WHEN THEY INSULT AND PERSECUTE YOU BECAUSE YOU BELIEVE IN ME...REJOICE ON THAT DAY, FOR YOUR REWARD WILL BE GREAT IN HEAVEN."

- ☐ Loyalty to Jesus, even when YOU are rejected because of it, will lead YOU to Heaven.

"BLESSED ARE THOSE WHO HEAR THE WORD OF GOD AND OBEY IT."

- ☐ YOU need to live YOUR faith every day, not just in your head, but in what you do, say ad in the choices YOU make.

DISCIPLESHIP

"ASK AND YOU WILL REVEIVE, KNOCK AND THE DOOR WILL BE OPENED TO YOU."

- ☐ Jesus really wants YOU to seek and know HIM.

"IF YOU WISH TO COME AFTER ME, DENY YOURSELF, PICK UP YOUR CROSS, AND FOLLOW ME."

- ☐ To know Jesus, YOU need to make time for HIM.

"WHOEVER WISHES TO SAVE THEIR LIFE WILL LOSE IT, BUT WHOEVER LOSES THEIR LIFE FOR MY SAKE WILL SAVE IT."

☐ YOU need to let Jesus take charge of your life.

"WHAT PROFIT IS IT FOR YOU TO GAIN THE WHOLE WORLD AND LOSE YOUR SOUL?"

☐ Money, power, pleasure, things will never satisfy YOU.

"YOU CANNOT SERVE GOD AND MONEY. YOU WILL LOVE THE ONE AND HATE THE OTHER."

☐ Money, power, things can make you greedy and selfish.

"SEEK FIRST THE KINGDOM OF GOD AND ALL THINGS WILL BE GIVEN UNTO YOU."

☐ When YOU face problems and suffering, go to the Lord first.

SUFFERING

"IF YOU SHOULD SUFFER FOR WHAT IS RIGHT, YOU ARE BLESSED!"

☐ YOU are like Jesus and will have eternal life for doing what is right.

"SUFFERING PRODUCES PERSEVERENCE. PERSEVERENCE PRODUCES CHARACTER; AND CHARACTER GIVES HOPE."

☐ No pain, no gain!

"WHILE YOU ARE IN THE WORLD, YOU WILL SUFFER, BUT DON'T BE AFRAID FOR I HAVE OVERCOME THE FEAR OF SUFFERING AND DEATH."

☐ Jesus is with YOU in your suffering and will help YOU overcome your fear of it, as He did His.
☐ If YOU suffer like Jesus, YOU will raise up like Jesus.

"OUR SUFFERINGS MAKE UP FOR WHAT IS LACKING IN JESUS' SUFFERINGS."

☐ YOUR suffering can help others, like Jesus' did for YOU and the world.

"THE SUFFERINGS OF THE PRESENT ARE NOTHING COMPARED TO THE GLORY THAT WILL BE OURS."

☐ I can't even begin to imagine Heaven's greatness, but the Lord wants YOU to have fun doing it, because it is the future He has planned for YOU.

WORDS TO LIVE BY

"DO UNTO OTHERS WHAT YOU WOULD HAVE THEM DO UNTO YOU."

☐ Respect and be good to people.

"DO NOT JUDGE OTHER PEOPLE, AND GOD WILL NOT JUDGE YOU."

☐ Refrain from the gossip, racism, and prejudice.

"DON'T STORE YOUR TREASURE HERE ON EARTH WHERE RUST AND MOTH WILL DEVOUR THEM."

☐ Power and material things will never make YOU happy. Experiencing Jesus and having a dialogue relationship with God will.

"WHERE YOUR TREASURE IS, THERE ALSO IS YOUR HEART."

☐ What YOUR values are will affect who and what YOU are.

"DO NOT LIVE BY BREAD ALONE BUT BY EVERY WORD THAT COMES FROM GOD."

☐ Pleasure and things aren't the important things in life. God and people are.

"THE COMMANDMENT I LEAVE YOU IS THIS, LOVE ONE ANOTHER AS I HAVE LOVED YOU."

☐ Jesus wants YOU to be compassionate and caring.

"THE TRUE CHILDREN OF GOD ARE THOSE WHO LET GOD'S SPIRIT LEAD THEM."

☐ YOU can experience Jesus revealing His will to YOU every day.

"BE COMPASSIONATE AS YOUR HEAVENLY FATHER IS COMPASSIONATE."

☐ I want YOU to be sensitive to the poor, needy, and people who are hurting, even people you don't like.

"IF ANYONE ACKNOWLEDGES THAT JESUS IS THE SON OF GOD, GOD LIVES IN YOU AND YOU ARE IN GOD."

☐ YOU can experience Jesus revealing His will to YOU every day.
☐ When you really mean it when you say that YOU love Jesus, YOU experience Him.

FLESH & SPIRIT

"THE DESIRES OF THE FLESH ARE AGAINST THE DESIRES OF THE SPIRIT."

☐ There are evil actions that hurt YOU badly and can cause deep emotional wounds.

"FROM THE FLESH COMES Fornication, Impurity, Free License, Idolatry, Sorcery, Enmity, Strife, Jealousy, Anger, Selfishness, Dissension, Envy, Drunkenness, And Carousing."

- ☐ Those Who Do Such Things Will Not Inherit the "Kingdom Of God."
- ☐ These violate and harm YOUR mind, body, and spirit.

HOW WE GET TO HEAVEN

"COME BLESSED OF MY FATHER, INHERIT THE KINGDOM PREPARED FOR YOU."

- ☐ I was HUNGRY, and you gave me something to EAT.
- ☐ I was THIRSTY, and you gave me a DRINK.
- ☐ I was a STRANGER, and you WELCOMED me.
- ☐ I was NAKED, and you CLOTHED me.
- ☐ I was SICK, and you CARED for me.
- ☐ I was in PRISON, and you VISITED me.

As often as YOU do these things to the least of my brothers and sisters, you are doing it to me.

GOD'S LOVE FOR US

"I, THE LORD, TAKE GREAT DELIGHT IN YOU. I WILL NOT TAKE MY LOVE FOR YOU AWAY."

- ☐ Of all creation, YOU are God's favorite.

"BEFORE YOU WERE KNIT IN YOUR MOTHER'S WOMB, I KNEW YOU AND LOVED YOU."

- ☐ God created YOU, and Heaven is YOUR real home.

"I NO LONGER CALL YOU SERVANTS, BUT NOW I CALL YOU MY FRIENDS."

- ☐ God wants a "friendship relationship" with YOU.

FEAR

"DO NOT BE AFRAID, FOR I AM WITH YOU EVERYDAY UNTIL THE END OF TIME."

- ☐ When YOU focus off of your problems and focus on My presence with you, I, your Lord, will drive your fears away.

"GOD IS YOUR REFUGE AND STRENGTH."

- ☐ God will give you inner peace even in YOUR suffering.

"WHERE THERE IS FEAR, LOVE HAS NOT REACHED PERFECTION, FOR LOVE DISPELS FEAR."

- ☐ If you stay in your fear, you have not experienced the Lord's LOVE.

"THE LORD DISCIPLINES YOU, BECAUSE HE LOVES YOU."

- ☐ Jesus wants YOU to grow and deliver YOU from those things that inhibit that growth.

ANGER

"A QUICK TEMPERED PERSON DOES FOOLISH THINGS."

- ☐ Anger can stir up dissension, because YOU will want to punish instead of forgive and communicate.
- ☐ YOU should be quick to listen, slow to speak, and slow to be angry.

"IN YOUR ANGER, DO NOT SIN."

- [ ] When YOUR anger wants to punish and hurt the other, it is YOUR sin.

"DO NOT OVERCOME EVIL WITH EVIL, BUT OVERCOME IT WITH GOOD."

- [ ] Don't seek revenge. Love YOUR enemies.

"RID YOURSELVES OF ANGER, RAGE, SLANDER, AND FILTHY LANGUAGE."

- [ ] These degrade YOU and others.

"BE KIND AND COMPASSIONATE, FORGIVING EACH OTHER, JUST AS JESUS FORGAVE YOU."

- [ ] YOU make mistakes, too.

"DO NOT LET THE SUN GO DOWN ON YOUR ANGER."

- [ ] Ask and give forgiveness quickly.

GUILT

"IF YOU FORGIVE OTHERS WHEN THEY SIN, GOD WILL FORGIVE YOU WHEN YOU SIN."

- [ ] The Lord wants YOU to free others and help them to change.

"EVERYONE WHO BELIEVES IN JESUS RECEIVES THE FORGIVENESS OF SINS."

- [ ] Jesus wants to free YOU from sin and to be happy.

"YOUR SINS WILL BE AS FAR AS THE EAST IS FROM THE WEST."

- [ ] Jesus not only forgives YOUR sins but forgets what YOU did.

RESURRECTION AND DEATH

"I AM THE RESURECTION AND THE LIFE. IF YOU BELIEVE IN ME, EVEN IF YOUR BODY DIES, YOU SHALL LIVE."

- ☐ There is no such thing as death and the end of YOU.

"WHOEVER EATS MY FLESH AND DRINKS MY BLOOD SHALL HAVE ETERNAL LIFE."

- ☐ Jesus' presence in YOUR life through prayer and faith in the Eucharist is the ticket to YOUR eternal life.

"IF WE LIVE WITH CHRIST AND DIE WITH CHRIST, WE SHALL BE RAISED WITH HIM."

- ☐ The Lord wants YOU to be aware that HE is with you every day, teaching you how to live, according to His will.

CHAPTER 16:
REFLECTIONS-PRAYERS-PRESENTATIONS & RITUALS
(Mine, not Jesus', so don't blame Him!)

EXPERIENCING THE HOLY SPIRIT
& DISCERNMENT

By Francis Pompei, OFM | May 18, 2016

A presentation I gave on the Holy Spirit, how it affects our lives, and knowing the difference between what is from me and what is from the Holy Spirit. I thought it might help you, too.

Who knows what ya gonna do when the Holy Ghost gets inside ya! Do I hear an Amen?

(My Baptist minister friend, Ernie, ended all his sermons with this. He sure had the wisdom and gift!)

As we think about Pentecost, it is important to realize that the Holy Spirit is an experience, not a theology. To help understand what Jesus said and where we fit in, here are some ideas that I hope are helpful and perhaps thought provoking.

The fulfillment of salvation is not just the incarnation, not just Jesus' teachings, his Suffering, Death, Resurrection, his forgiveness, his conquering of Death and Evil, but the restoration and free gift of experiencing the Unconditional Love of God that completes the divine void in us.

According to Scripture, the early Christians and the new covenant are all centered on the Holy Spirit. Here are some examples:

- ☐ *I will place my Spirit within them and write the law upon their hearts. (Jer. 31:33)*
- ☐ *Wait here for the fulfillment of my Father's promise. He will send you the Holy Spirit, the advocate, who will teach you all things. (Jn. 14:26)*
- ☐ *They were all filled with the Holy Spirit and began to witness boldly and without fear. (Acts 2:4)*
- ☐ *The place where they prayed shook, because they were all filled with (experienced) the Holy Spirit. (Acts 4:31)*
- ☐ *It is the Spirit that gives life. (Jn. 6:63)*
- ☐ *How much more will your Heavenly Father give the Holy Spirit to those who ask? (Lk. 11:13)*

OUR GOAL AND DAILY ASSIGNMENT IS

- ☐ To learn how to experience the Holy Spirit.
- ☐ To learn how the Spirit reveals God's Will.
- ☐ To learn how to discern the Spirit, what is from us, and what is from the Lord.
- ☐ To know the difference between our thoughts and will and the Spirit's.
- ☐ To learn how to let go of my will and seek God's will every day, all day.

"It is no longer I who live, but Christ Jesus who lives in me."

When we do this, we can experience the salvation of the Lord and the way He liberates us from the old way of the law and the world's way. He renews us by "putting on the mind of Christ," as St. Paul says. (1 Cor. 2:16)

HOW DOES THE HOLY SPIRIT AFFECT US?

Senior woman (a widow): "It's hard to explain what it feels like to actually experience and feel God's love in you. My husband died five years ago, and the loneliness was unbearable, but I'm not alone any more. Thank you, Jesus."

Parish staff member: "We are not just another parish staff, council or meeting. Experiencing the Holy Spirit with and in each other when we pray has created us into a family. Isn't that what Church is supposed to be?"

Teenager: "Praying and talking to Jesus with the other kids is where I found and experience God. Jesus helps me big time with my decisions and guides me through tough times. He has become my best friend and is always there for me."

Teenager: "I talk with Jesus all the time — in school, when I'm on the football field, and when I have problems. He always listens to me and gets me through all my problems, even if they don't work out the way I want them to. I wish someone would have taught me how to pray and live this way when I was younger."

A Young Teenage Woman, 19, an addict and prostitute. "I experience Jesus out here with me on the streets. I know He loves me, and He is the only thing that keeps me going."

Young couple: "We talk to Jesus every day, and many times we experience the Holy Spirit and Unconditional Love of God for us as we look into each other's eyes. We really experience being one with Him and each other. If only all married couples were taught to do this."

Adult man: "Experiencing the Holy Spirit is indescribable. I have never felt so complete in my life."

Men's group: "Experiencing Jesus on a regular basis with other likeminded men has been a Godsend for all of us. The Holy Spirit continues to teach us — through the scriptures and through each other — how to be better men, disciples of Jesus, husbands, and fathers. All of us thought we were doing pretty well when it came to going to church and faith, but experiencing Jesus and the Holy Spirit has turned us 180 degrees in our relationship with the Lord and how we live our daily lives."

The Lord tells us to let go of what we think and want to do and let the Holy Spirit reveal His plan and will for us. Jesus is teaching us to think, live and pray this way.

- "I have come to do the will of my Father." *(Jn. 6:38-39)*
- "Father, not according to my will, but your will." *(Lk. 22:42)*
- "Thy kingdom come, Thy will be done." *(Mt. 6:9-13)*

DISCERNING THE LORD'S WILL

What all of us need to let go of continually is our focus on ourselves, especially at meetings dealing with policy making, problems, situations, and issues. Instead, we need to focus on the Holy Spirit and learn **HOW** the Spirit reveals the Lord's will. It is

- Not a democracy where the majority wins.
- Not who has the best idea and can convince others
- Not always the most practical, efficient, or logical idea
- Not always the way we were taught.
- Not just because it's a good idea.

- Not always because it's the way we've always done it.
- Not always because it is the safest way and a way that I'm comfortable with or can control.
- Not always because it worked in the past.
- Not always because it's a theologically correct idea, ritual, or service.
- Not always because I am the pope, bishop, pastor, deacon, religious, director, or person with authority.

JESUS OPPOSED THESE MENTALITIES:

- "My ways are not your ways, says the Lord." *(Isaiah 55:8-9)*
- "You treat man made laws as if they were God's commandments." *(Mt. 23:16)*
- "Do not hold your authority over people like the Pharisees." *(Mt. 20:25)*
- "You put heavy burdens on people but do not lift a finger to help anyone." *(Mt. 23:4)*
- "If the fig tree does not bear fruit, cut it down." *(Lk. 13:9)*

From what Jesus said about the Holy Spirit as the fulfillment of his Father's promise, He's telling us it's not just enough to believe in Him or go to church and live good lives, but to experience intimacy with Him through the Holy Spirit, like they did on Pentecost. He never ceases to invite us to have a personal daily relationship with Him and experience Him with others— whenever two or three of us gather, in his name.

On a personal note, I cannot teach others what I, myself, have never been taught or experienced. I think that followers of Jesus need to learn what to do specifically to **experience** the Lord and the Holy Spirit whenever gathered, **regardless of our individual preference or spirituality.**

The true test that would indicate we are on the right path is, every time we meet, the room should "shake" because we experience the presence of the Lord who said, "I will never abandon you and will be with you every day until the end of time." Praise you, Jesus, Hallelujah!

THE "ROMAN" CATHOLIC CHURCH
PAST, PRESENT, AND TOMORROW

How did we get here &
A "Way Forward" prophecy

As a Franciscan Catholic Priest, I put this together as a "Reflection of Hope" in the midst of all the sexual abuse, cover-ups, and corruption in the Hierarchy of the Church and the horrific suffering caused throughout history and in the present. NOTE: The underlying point is that the Evil that has infected the "Roman" Catholic Church is the same Evil that affects governments, all religions and institutions when unbridled power is appropriated in the hands of a few or one person, instead of from, by, and of God. Evil has enslaved human nature to POWER, "If you eat of this Tree, you will become like God." (Gen. 3:5)

When I professed my vows as a Franciscan, poverty, chastity, and obedience—part of the Ritual was to "Resist POWER in all of its forms." The way the world is now, I know why. What else I know is that LOVE is greater than Power.

JESUS SAID,

Acts 1:8
You will receive power when the Holy Spirit comes upon you, and you will be my witnesses in Jerusalem, and in all Judea and Samaria, and to the ends of the earth.

John 14:26
The Advocate, the Holy Spirit, whom the Father will send in my name, will teach you **all** things and will **remind** you of everything I have told you.

PENTECOST: They were all (men and women) filled with the Holy Spirit, praised God in tongues, and then went out unafraid, witnessing and proclaiming Christ crucified.

THE HOLY SPIRIT: Trying to describe the Holy Spirit in theological human words is to violate whom the Holy Spirit is. It's like trying to scientifically describe the experience of love. It is impossible. God, including God the Holy Spirit, cannot and will never be defined or confined. The only way to know God, Father, Son, and Holy Spirit, is not in the mind, but in our spirit and soul, by experiencing the divine and becoming one with God.

JESUS' PRAYER FOR ALL BELIEVERS

*"Father, I pray that all of them may be one, as you, Father, are **in** me, and I am **in** you. May they also be **in** us, so that the world may believe that you sent Me. I have given them the glory that you gave Me, so that they may be one, as we are one. I **in** them and you in me—that they may be perfectly united, so that the world may know that you sent me and have loved them just as you have loved me." (Jn. 17:22)*

According to Jesus, the Holy Spirit is becoming one with and experiencing the Unconditional Love and Wisdom of God. Anyone baptized by the Holy Spirit cannot use words to adequately describe the experience, because the Holy Spirit and the Divine are not known by thoughts or theology, but by experiencing God's love revealing Himself and becoming intimately one with Him, as described in John's gospel. This is why the crowd who gathered outside the upper room, listening to the apostles and followers of Jesus speak and witness in various languages, thought they were drunk.

EARLY CHRISTIANS:

This was the whole purpose of Jesus coming, that the God who created us, loves us, and is now not only with us, but can be experienced in us, and in one another. Becoming one with and loving one another is the driving power of the Holy Spirit, as described by Jesus in John's gospel, *"...that they become one. Then the world will know you sent me by the way they love one another." (Jn. 17:23)*

The experience of the Holy Spirit and the Risen Christ was now the goal each day. They were taught, guided, healed, forgiven and delivered by the Lord. That is why they gathered together, for no other purpose than to experience the Holy Spirit and the Lord with them. From that experience, the Lord created them into his family, loving and ministering to one another.

"Unless the Lord build the city, the laborers labor in vain" (Ps. 127:1) **not a program, not who has the best idea or who has the office, but the Holy Spirit—the true vicar of Christ, the one who stands in His place.**

"Whenever two or three are gathered in my name, there I will dwell in their midst." (Mt. 18:20)

THE POINT HERE IS that they experienced their Creator and Father, their Lord, the Risen Christ. *"...and the house where they prayed shook, because they were all filled with the Holy Spirit and spoke in tongues, and their numbers increased." (Acts 4:31)*

In order to love one another, the Holy Spirit granted them the gifts of the Spirit, to lead (*Apostoloi*, Greek for leader), discern the Spirit (*Prophets*), teach, preach, preside at the breaking of the bread, heal (anoint), perform miracles, and lesser gifts, words of knowledge, deliverance, and the least, praising the Lord in tongues.

The first mentioned gifts provided leadership, guidance, and wisdom for the communities, the latter to encourage, heal, support, and love one another, by sacrificing themselves for each other.

WHO AND HOW WERE PEOPLE APPOINTED TO THESE MINISTRIES? The believers in each community appointed them. How did they do that, by their experiencing who had been given and manifested the gift of the Holy Spirit. In other words, they shared with their community the experience of a specific person's gift of the Holy Spirit, "When 'Junia' came and prayed over me, I could feel the Holy Spirit in her embracing me." Others in the community would speak up and confirm that they too experienced the same when "Junia" prayed.

Then the leader (Apostle) and the Prophets *(who discerned and experienced that their sister or brother had been given the gifts of the Holy Spirit)* would appoint and designate them to the ministry and the Office. Different gifts were given to different people, but all by the same Spirit—one not being greater than another. This equality was specifically described in St. Paul's epistles, "...many gifts, but One Spirit."

The selection and appointment was **not** by a democratic vote nor by whom had the most influence, and more importantly not by everyone who desired or wanted the Office.

The community decided by their experience of the gift of the Holy Spirit in certain people, whether it be healing, teaching, preaching, deliverance, or discernment. Then the prophets and leader *(who had the gift of discernment of the Spirit)* would confirm the community's experience by appointing the person(s) to the office(s) in their Church family.

EARLY CHURCH FATHERS: As Christianity flourished in the East and West, more and more small communities were established by the experience and guidance of the Holy Spirit. As the faith spread and evolved, the Church faced more and more heresies questioning who Jesus was, what He was, and even how He was. Therefore, the leaders *(Apostles)* of local churches began to put into human words who Jesus was, what He was, how He was, and what constitutes the absolutes of our faith.

This is called the "Apostles' Creed." It is what makes us Christians, and in our tradition—Catholic. Their teaching was like all teachings of the Church, based upon the believer's experience of the Holy Spirit. **It is the Holy Spirit, again, that is the source of all teaching and guidance, not man.**

Jesus himself condemned this method in the Pharisees, *You make man's laws equal to God's commandments and put heavy burdens on people and won't lift of finger to help them... blind guides, hypocrites, all! (Mt. 23:4)*

THE ROMAN EMPIRE: When Constantine, the emperor, converted to Christianity, it gradually spread throughout the Empire. This was a positive influence on the faith, which helped to spread the gospel throughout the world. However, the Christian faith was now the religion of the empire, meaning that changes gradually occurred. People across the Empire were coerced and pressured to conform to the new religion. This initiated that Christianity become more and more— a "religion," instead of a movement of the Holy Spirit. As the Church grew in numbers, it represented the end of small basic communities being personal and more individualistic in worship, emphasizing the **Mystery** of God instead of the experience of the Holy Spirit. The breaking of the bread slowly became something to be observed and not participated in, without sharing it in the course of a meal like the early Christians.

THE "ROMAN" CATHOLIC CHURCH: As the Church grew, like all humans, it was tempted by Original Sin to appropriate power and authority to itself, to be like God— the dispensers of the divine. The Roman Empire imposed its government structure on Christianity, placing the Holy Spirit under the umbrella and protection of the government, which seemed to be a welcomed opportunity to appease both the spiritual needs of the people, but more conveniently the political.

This kind of reasoning opened the door for **Evil**, as it did in the Garden of Eden, for authority, power, and the gifts of the Holy Spirit to be in the hands of men who occupied appointed offices only. A bishop alone could now discern the Holy Spirit; only a priest could anoint and preside at Eucharist and hear confessions; and only deacons and priests could preach, perform marriages and bless. The major point here is now the gifts of the Holy Spirit were no longer given to whomever the Spirit chose, but only to those who held the government appointed offices—**the pope, local bishops, pastors, and local clergy.** The "Roman" Catholic Church became another institutionalized religion, with the dissemination of the Holy Spirit in human hands.

"Power corrupts, and absolute power absolutely corrupts."

Despite this appropriation of the Holy Spirit, the Spirit has done great and miraculous things over the centuries by those who had the gifts of the Holy Spirit and lived by faith. At the same time, the corruption of the system by people who had the offices, *but not the gift*, resulted in corruption within the papacy, the episcopacy, the clergy, and the believers. This resulted in crusades, schisms, wars, inquisitions, murder, rape, sexual abuse, genocide, the Reformation, and the list goes on.

Granted we are all sinners, but I wonder if all Christian denominations would have sinned less and loved more if their daily guide was their experience of Jesus and the Holy Spirit in themselves. I wonder if there would be more love whenever they gathered together with their sisters and brothers to be filled with God's embrace. I wonder if we experienced the Holy Spirit, through acknowledging one another's gifts, would we have bonded more in mutual and caring love, like the early Christians.

I wonder if we would have healed and forgiven each other more, and settled our differences because we will have learned how to by the Holy Spirit.

I was just wondering! What do think?

<u>CONCLUSION</u>:

I am not a heretic, a rebel, a Conservative, or radical Liberal. I am "baptized" with the Holy Spirit as a Catholic, and with all my heart believe every word in the Apostles' Creed as the absolute truth. I also believe in the leadership offices and ministries of the Catholic Church. I stand with all believers together with the Holy Father, shepherds, priests, prophets, teachers, preachers, healers, those with the gift of discernment, and words of knowledge.

As I watch the leadership and institutional structures of the "Roman" Catholic Church fall and dry up like an old wine skin, from the sexual abuse of minors, nuns, and others to cover-ups by bishops and staff, I must confess that after 45 years of priesthood, I sometimes am ashamed of being a **Roman** Catholic priest. The Roman Empire's superimposed government structure on early Christianity's trust and reliance on the Holy Spirit and the gifts of the Spirit has not only let evil in, but it has led us to the corruption that the Catholic Church is currently in. Yet, I trust and know that the Holy Spirit will rise from the ashes, and the new wine will spring forth in a new wine skin.

I believe that the new wine will flow when we, like our evangelical brothers and sisters, who are flourishing *(with many former Catholics joining)* and are being granted the gifts of the Holy Spirit, empowered to use them. They are on fire, because they have been baptized by the Holy Spirit, like the disciples were at Pentecost and Paul on the road to Damascus. I believe all Christians of today, of any denomination, who put the experience and gifts of the Holy Spirit at the center of their worship and community will bear much "fruit." I believe, like the early Christians, that only those who have the gifts of the Spirit, as experienced, discerned, and recognized by the whole community are given the office, **instead of all the gifts residing in one person** who may not have the necessary gift(s) to exercise their office and ministry.

In short, **Pope John the XXIII** was the real "prophet" for these end times by proclaiming that the Church needed a **New Pentecost.** The Ecumenical Council involved other religions, people from all walks of society, to discern God's will— not only for the Catholic Church, but the whole world. I also believe, because we have not listened and discerned the direction of the Holy Spirit in these past

50 years, our leadership and the institutional church established by the Roman Empire, is in the destruction that they (and we) have created.

There is no need to be offended, defensive, or guilty by all this; instead, choose to trust in the Lord; letting go of the old wine skin, the power, control, and structures that guided us for centuries but that aren't bearing fruit any more. Jesus said, "If the fig tree does not bear fruit, cut it down." **In other words, stop doing it that way**. Look forward, keeping your spiritual ears and eyes open for the movements of the Holy Spirit that will always bear fruit.

I am convinced a new outpouring of the Holy Spirit is coming, and it is coming like a strong driving wind and roaring fire with gifts and power to confront Satan and evil forces that are creating chaos, seducing many believers and seeking to destroy our faith and Church.

Remember there are two baptisms—the baptism of water and the baptism of the Holy Spirit. If you have not experienced the baptism of the Holy Spirit, like they did at Pentecost when the early Christians gathered and the room shook, then keep praying and ask for it. When you and all in your community and parish do, you are on the greatest journey and adventure of your lives that ends with eternal life.

I Say "Alleluia" & Come "Holy Spirit"

A PROPHECY

*The new Catholic Church will rise when the family of believers meet in Rome with the Holy Father and the shepherds to be renewed in their faith, by being baptized with and **experiencing the Holy Spirit** in a new Pentecost.*

*Then it shall be given them all the **"gift of discernment," distinguishing what is from man and what is from the Lord, and without question or doubt, breaking all factions and those things that divide us.** And the place where they have assembled will shake with praises of God in their midst as a new **"fire"** will come upon them and awaken their hearts. There will be an outpouring of forgiveness, healing and deliverance from all the divisions, half-truths, lies and corruption that have infected the Lord's servants and family. There will be no more liberals, conservatives, radicals, or rebels **as they will rejoice in the Holy Spirit as One,** and then they shall raise a mighty roar of voices praising the Lord, as on the day of Pentecost.*

*And the Lord will bestow the gifts of the Holy Spirit, not only on the assembled, but on all believers throughout the world, as many have already been given but not acknowledged. Believers will no longer pray for vocations, but for the gifts of the Holy Spirit to be bestowed on their sisters and brothers. And the great **Gift of Discernment,** forgotten and lost by many for centuries will be given, and the floodgates of shepherds, leaders, and ministry will be opened once again as Jesus proclaimed.*

*"...and **these signs** shall **follow all** that **believers** in my name shall cast out devils; they shall speak with new tongues; they shall take up serpents; and if they drink any deadly thing, it shall not hurt **them**; they shall lay hands on the sick, and they shall recover." (Mark)*

*And the Holy Spirit will no longer reside in the hands of a few, but flourish like the wind. The communities of believers will be led and ministered to by their own sisters and brothers who have been given the gifts of the Holy Spirit, recognized and **experienced by their own church family.** Their numbers will increase, and they will flourish like the palm tree. The mighty and all-powerful Lord, the Risen Christ, will rejoice in the Holy Spirit as He did when the apostles returned from their mission empowered with authority to preach, heal, forgive, and deliver. God's words and promise that the "gates of hell will not prevail over his people and church" will be fulfilled.*

*Then the power and Unconditional Love of the Risen Christ in the Eucharist will emanate to all gathered at His table, and just as He suffered, was broken and died, so will have His church. But as He rose from the dead, so shall we His church, the people of God, His people, and the Father **"Dance!"***

"See, I Am Making All Things New."

OUR CATHOLIC FAITH

IS A 'HOO-RAH'

My brother who is a Diocesan priest put the following talk together. It spells out our unique tradition that has evolved over 2000 years. It celebrates the wonderful spirituality of our sisters and brothers within our Catholic faith.

YOU CATHOLICS ARE STRANGE AND A TAD CRAZY

from the words of a non-Catholic

YOU CATHOLICS have prayer cards, pictures, statues, and medals.

YOU GET FRESH PALM LEAVES just before Easter and make crosses and other religious symbols out of them. Then a year later, you burn them, and on a certain Wednesday you put their ashes on your foreheads to walk around in public letting everyone know you are sinners...and repenting your sins.

YOU HAVE THIS STRING OF DIFFERENT SIZE BEADS tied together with a cross at one end. You repeat the same prayer over and over to a woman named Mary, whom you claim gave birth to God while still a virgin. You call her the mother of God, and you call the beads *the rosary* and believe this prayer leads you closer to God.

YOU BLESS WATER, and you believe that God will protect you if you make the sign of the cross on your forehead with it, because it reminds you that He is with you.

YOU SPRINKLE THIS WATER on almost anything–dogs, cats, horses, fish, rabbits, trucks, cars, boats, even children's stuffed animals, and believe that this makes them blessed and special not only to you but to God.

YOU LIGHT COLORED CANDLES and place them in front of pictures, icons, and statues for specific reasons, needs, requests, trusting that God will answer and be with you.

YOU DON'T BELIEVE IN GHOSTS; nevertheless, you ask favors of people who have died. Because you believe they are not dead but alive with God in Heaven, they can intercede for you and inspire you.

YOU CONFESS YOUR SINS TO ANOTHER HUMAN BEING and believe

that this human being's forgiveness is God's forgiveness and is also the forgiveness of your church family, all at the same time.

YOU LOVE RITUAL, IMAGERY, STATUES AND PICTURES that remind you of holy people who have gone before you that you claim to experience the mystery of God's presence and love in and through them.

YOU SAY THAT YOU RECEIVE JESUS AS YOUR FOOD AND DRINK through something that looks like, feels like, tastes like bread and wine, but it isn't. You say it really is the body and blood and Unconditional Love of the risen Lord who said he would never abandon you—your risen Christ in the Eucharist, not just a memory of the last supper 2000 years ago, but really Him, in a unique and loving way.

WHAT'S REALLY STRANGE is while the world is having happy hours, you are making holy hours. You spend time sitting in front of a brass box you call a tabernacle, claiming your risen Jesus lives in that bread. Then you say that by the end of the hour, no matter what you're worried about or what your problems are, that His being with you gives you Peace of Mind and rest, when nothing else does. I don't see any other Christian churches doing this, only you Catholics.

THEN I WATCH YOU, NOT ONLY LOVING GOD, but loving one another, even though you are sinners like everyone else, claiming that this is what Jesus asks you to do—that the Catholic Church is not a museum of saints, but a hospital for sinners.

YOU CATHOLICS ARE REALLY STRANGE, but I must admit that all these things you do that make you "Catholic" **makes me wonder if I am missing out on something wonderful from God.**

I SAY HOO-RAH TO THE CATHOLIC FAITH!

CREATION

Stewards, Not Abusers

In response to Pope Francis' document **Laudatu** *Si concerning the Church's concern for the Environment and Creation, I put the following together from a keynote, research presentation I gave at the University of Washington in the State of Washington on the Spiritual Benefits of Nature.*

I've been a backcountry hiker since college at the Olympics, American/Canadian Rockies, Zion, Cascades, Rainier, Italian Alps, Highlands of Scotland and countless other areas in the United States.

"Only in the last moment of human history has the delusion arisen that human beings can flourish apart from the rest of the living world" *(Wilson, 1992).*

"We spend more than 95%-99% of our adult lives—indoors, cloistered from nature, 'disconnected humans' from our sensory experience of nature, and we lose both the experience of feeling fulfilled and the wisdom nature provides. The result is our need for fulfillment overcomes our sense of reason and we want and want and want, and there is never enough. Instead, we obtain momentary satisfaction and pleasure from money, power, pleasure, and things, and even unhealthy relationships that we know are personally and environmentally destructive, and in the end produce only stress, depression, dependency, broken relationships, poverty and mass conflict. **This mentality and behavior is the definition of addiction and insanity, to knowingly destroy our life support system, and our biological/psychological roots**" *(Cohen, 1992).*

Several religions have given the wilderness different meanings:

- ☐ Wilderness signified an environment to draw closer to God.
- ☐ Wilderness represented a sanctuary from the evils of society, a testing ground where people are cleansed, humbled, refreshed, and made ready for the future.

SPIRITUAL BENEFITS OF THE WILDERNESS AND NATURE

1. Gives us a sense of belonging to a unified, animated, spiritually encompassing world of trees, animals, large and small. It brings

176

us close to vegetation, flowers, even the water and air that gives us life.

2. Inspires the arts, music, poetry and literature.

3. Has the power to heal, give rest and Peace of Mind, body, and spirit. Peace of Mind is a prerequisite to peace in our families, communities and the world.

4. Can dissipate stress, violence, and prejudice. It can even reduce or eliminate dependencies.

5. Can raise and answer the deepest questions of the meaning of our human existence, who and what we are, and where we come from. Through nature we can experience the Creator's Spirit in it, and as created realities ourselves, we can experience God in us.

6. Grief, raging feelings, defeats, and frustrations of our everyday lives seem less painful and important when we are in nature…. **It's called "sanity**."

7. We are the dependent members of the great community of life. Storms, great floods, avalanches, immensity of space all demand respect. They remind us of our comparative weakness, vulnerability, and our **sense of dependence, resulting in an attitude of responsibility and indebtedness** for sustenance from the oxygen, water from the rivers, lakes and streams to the food, shelter, clothing and medicines that it provides.

8. **Solitude**: Wilderness' solitude is a state of mind, experiencing no reminders of society, its inventions, and conventions. This includes being constantly surrounded by people, mechanization, unnatural noise, signs, and manmade artifacts.

This experience of solitude is what I call the "cosmic, self-awareness, the God Zone," where the Divine and we can meet and commune as one. It is the place where who we are and what we are is revealed and experienced. This in turn can lead to the physical, psychological and spiritual benefits, and to the experience of the Divine.

As St. Francis of Assisi, the Patron Saint of Creation and the

Environment, experienced, *"I am God's creature; of Him I am part; I feel His love awakening my heart."*

PRAISE GOD WITH CREATION PRAYER

Bless The Lord, All You Works Of The Lord. Praise And Exalt Him Above All Forever. *(from the Psalms)*

R: *Praise the Lord.*

- ☐ All You Angels and Heavenly Hosts... ***Praise the Lord.***
- ☐ You Heavens Above...*R.*
- ☐ All You Waters Above The Heavens...*R.*
- ☐ Sun and Moon...*R.*
- ☐ Stars of Heaven...*R.*
- ☐ Every Shower and Dew...*R.*
- ☐ All You Winds And Air...*R.*
- ☐ Fire and Heat...*R.*
- ☐ Dew and Rain...*R.*
- ☐ Frost and Chill... Ice and Snow...*R.*
- ☐ Nights and Days... Light and Darkness...*R.*
- ☐ Lightning and Clouds...*R.*
- ☐ Mountains and Hills...*R.*
- ☐ Everything Growing From The Earth...*R.*
- ☐ You Springs and Fountains...*R.*
- ☐ Seas and Rivers...*R.*
- ☐ You Dolphins... All Water Creatures...*R.*
- ☐ All You Birds Of The Air...*R.*
- ☐ Let All Creatures On The Earth...*R.*
- ☐ All God's People...*R.*
- ☐ Let Everything That Has Breath and Life...*R.*

ALLELUIA!

RITUALS AND PRAYERS FOR PEACE OF MIND AND DELIVERANCE

#1 OVERWHELMED

*For when you are overwhelmed by very bad news or a traumatic situation... Your mind, emotions, and feelings may feel over the top and out of control.

*Peace be with you. **It's me, Jesus**, your Lord and most of all, your Friend. I've been waiting for you. **Take a deep breath and relax.**

I know you are overwhelmed, and your thoughts and feelings are out of control. You're frightened of what's happening to you and worried about what might happen today, tomorrow, and in the future.

You're trapped in the vicious circle of the thoughts that are threatening you, and you're trapped in the fear that is turning into stress and panic. Evil is attacking you, as it did Me on the cross. Evil is tempting you to doubt that I am with you, and your fear and suffering will never end.

*So take another deep breath to calm down ... **Take it!** Now, let me help you, and together we will stop the vicious circle.*

***Slowly Repeat My Words**, and let them relax your mind and body little by little, so you can focus on Me here with you.*

Be Still and Know that I am God...	***Pause 10 sec.***
Be Still and Know that I am...	***Pause 10 sec.***
Be Still and Know...	***Pause 10 sec.***
Be Still...	***Pause 10 sec.***
Be...	***Pause 15 sec.***

The anxiety you are experiencing is from the negative thoughts that have entered your mind. Thinking about them over and over again is how the evil powers of Fear, Panic, Doubt and Despair are taking control of your will, peace of mind, and possessing your attention, instead of being aware that I'm right here with you.

So what are the negative thoughts, half-truths and lies that are attacking you this time?...that your problems will get worse, that you won't be able to deal with them down the road, or that it will never end?

THESE THOUGHTS ARE THE REAL ENEMY. *Dwelling on them is taking you down the path to panic, doubt, and making you anxious.*

STOP IT! *Stop letting evil do this to you. Together, let's you and I deliver and cast out these evil thoughts that are attacking you.*

Trust me by praying these words:

☐ *"Your power, Jesus, is greater than the powers of evil and lies that are attacking me." (Pause 10 sec.)*

☐ *"In Your name, Jesus, and by the power of your blood, I bind and cast out Fear, Worry, Anxiety, Doubt and Despair. **These have no power over me. I belong to Jesus.**" (Pause 15 sec.)*

☐ *"Lord, I'm tired, and surrender everything to You... Give me peace of mind and **rest!**" (Pause 30 sec. to experience it)*

#2 HEALING, DELIVERANCE & LETTING GO PRAYER FOR EVERYONE

*Jesus, I pray **first for miracles and extraordinary healing**: full and complete healing for all physical, mental, and emotional illnesses, and the hurt from broken relationships. Move, transform, and heal them, Lord.*

I pray for all those things that may take time to heal. *I trust you with them, Lord. You will be with and in me, every moment of every day, giving me strength, patience, and hope until I are healed.*

*I pray, too, Jesus, **for those things that are chronic** and may never pass away. I think about and join my suffering to Yours on the cross, and draw your strength into myself to endure the pain I have right now until it subsides.*

Lord, I imagine and direct Your power to every cell in my body, especially where I am in pain, in my thoughts... feelings... and in my very soul.

Lord, I want to let go and give you anything that should not be in me, the fear and worry from what disease and illness have done and are doing to me, fear and worry from my problems that are stressing me out. They control my thoughts with doubts in You, and even despair.

I choose to give You the negative thoughts, guilt and temptations I have let in, because of what I have done, the hurt and anger from what others have said or done to me. I see and believe you are taking them from me to yourself right now.

*Jesus, I choose **not** to take them back by thinking about and dwelling on them anymore, but instead stay focused and **think about**:*

☐ *You, right here in me.*

☐ *One by one, I think about my family, my friends, who love and believe in me. I want to feel their strength, love and prayers.*

(Pause and picture them, and when you do, enjoy their presence.)

Lord, heal and transform everything that controls my body, mind and my spirit. Free me, Jesus, by taking them...

Thank you, Lord, for this Peace of Mind. Now I can undergo anything that comes my way and problems that I still have, but now without being afraid, worried, angry, or feeling the urge to fight or fix them with my own power and strength. Jesus, you said that You would be with me every day until the end of time. I'm counting on it, and when I'm being tempted by fear and its negative thoughts and lies, I will think of you right there in me, give them to you, and wait for your peace.

Now, Lord, I just want to sit still and stay with you for a while in peace.

(Take as much time as you need

#3 FAMILY OR GROUP PRAYER FOR HEALING AND PEACE

Jesus, it's good to be with You. We have come together as your family, to pray and ask you to heal and deliver us from our fears. We are also praying for physical, emotional and spiritual healing for ourselves, those we are worried about, who need Your healing, and our brothers and sisters here with us. Help us to trust in You, and give everything to You now, so You can heal and set us free.

*Jesus, give me the grace to focus my attention on you, right here with me in the Eucharist that is really you, my Risen Lord... **(Pause 30 sec.)** **Focus on the Lord who is here with you.***

Jesus, I am overwhelmed by my problems, Suffering and Fear, and I'm tired. I need this time with You and my sisters and brothers, to experience Your healing and Peace of Mind.

*Holy Spirit, the Unconditional Love and power of God, embrace and pass through every part of my body and mind, especially that area where there is brokenness and disease. **(Pause 30 sec.)** **Be specific, and see the Lord doing this for you, because He is!***

*Jesus, I am asking first for extraordinary healing, for anything that may be at the root of my physical illness. Heal my body, and make it whole again... **(Pause 30 sec.)***

*Heal the scars and pain others and life have caused me. **(Pause 30 sec.)** **Tell the Lord, be specific and then let go of them.***

181

Heal those images in my past when I was or may have been abused—memories that haunt and drag me down to self-hatred and depression whenever I relive them. Heal my memory of these images by experiencing You with me, when they happened, what you wanted to happen, and what you did not want to happen. Most of all Lord, embrace me with your Unconditional Love here in the Eucharist that I did not experience. This will replace those painful memories and put them to rest whenever they return.

(Pause 1 minute.) Be specific. This time focus on the Lord right there with you. See Him, go to Him, let Him love that pain right out of you, and finally put that memory to rest forever.

Jesus, I am also asking to give me patience for all those things that may take time to heal through medication, therapies, and counseling, and give me hope and Your strength to endure my suffering, as You did Yours.

Lord, take all the negative thoughts, evil half-truths and lies, that I have let into my mind, which are overwhelming me with stress, worry, and fear—fear that tempts me with doubt and even despair...take them right now, Lord. I give them to you... Tell Jesus what they are.

Through the intercession of you, the Blessed Mother, St. Michael, and St. Benedict, and in the name of You, the Risen Christ, my Lord and my friend, deliver me from

☐	*Fear, Doubt and Despair...*	*Bind and Cast it out*
☐	*Temptation and all Evil...*	*Bind and Cast it out*
☐	*Lust...*	*Bind and Cast it out*
☐	*Self-Righteousness*	*Bind and Cast it out*
☐	*Self-Hatred...*	*Bind and Cast it out*
☐	*Hatred and Revenge*	*Bind and Cast it out*

Instead, Jesus, I choose the TRUTH, that You are here with me, being with my sisters and brothers, enjoying life, and doing Your will. So give me the grace not to take any of these half-truths and lies back by thinking about or dwelling on them.

Instead Lord, replace any anger with compassion and a willingness to forgive others who hurt me. **(Pause 15 sec.)**

Replace my stress with Rest and Peace. **(Pause 15 sec.)**

Replace my worry about tomorrow and the future by staying in the present. **(Pause 15 sec.) Be still, and enjoy it.**

*Jesus, you said love dispels fear, so deliver my fears, not only with your love, but also by remembering **all the people** who do love me, believe in me, and support me.*

Slowly, picture those who love you one by one. Experience what it's like when you are with them, and enjoy it.

I pray also for my sisters and brothers here with me now. I'm praying for whatever healing they are asking for. Lord, give them Your strength, courage, and my support. Deliver them from fear and worry.

Sisters and Brothers, you are no longer alone. The Lord and we, your family, are with you.

Place your hand on the shoulder of the person next to you or in front of you, close your eyes, and quietly pray for them. *(Pause 30 sec.)*

Open your eyes, remove your hands and pray.

Jesus, may your healing and deliverance continue now and in the days to come. Into your hands Lord, I commend my spirit.

Now close your eyes, be still, and just BE with the Lord. Enjoy! Take as much time as you need. When the leader says to open your eyes and stand, trace the cross with your thumb on each other's forehead and say:

"The Lord Continue To Heal You. Peace be with you."

FINAL PRAYER: *Our Father who art in Heaven…*

Now enjoy your family, friends, and life, and don't take back any of the negative thoughts, half-truths, and lies. Stay in the present, aware of the lord with you, whether you experience Him or not. You're not alone. We are with you.

#4 MY DAILY TIME WITH JESUS PRAYER

Peace be with you. I've been with you waiting…waiting for you to spend time with me…just you and Me.

Perhaps you have let the broken world in again with all those negative thoughts, half-truths, and lies. You are trying to fix and control everything again by yourself, so you can feel safe, secure, and have some Peace of Mind.

Thinking about them over and over is what is causing your fear, worry, frustration and anxiety.

Relax, stop the vicious circle, and stop beating yourself up with guilt, self-doubts, and powerlessness. Just be with Me.

I want you to tell Me what has hurt you. And after you tell Me, let go of them, and don't take them back by dwelling on them anymore. This is the hardest thing for you to do, but the more you choose to do it, the easier and more natural it will become.

So take your time, be specific, and tell Me what's making you so anxious and stressing you out... tell Me... now let go of it... and let Me take care of it.

Now tell me who are the people and loved ones you are worrying about, and what's your prayer for them...?

If you're feeling guilty for anything you've done, anything you are ashamed of and hate yourself for, don't do that. Just tell me what you have done, ask for forgiveness and a new start, and it shall be yours....

So confess, and let me set you free.

*Lastly, ask and pray for anything, so **I can give you what you need**. Ask now, and you will receive even more than you asked for. But be patient and trust Me. Take your time. Ask now, I'm listening...*

Now take a deep breath... take it! Breathe in, and imagine grabbing hold of all the anxious thoughts in your head, the tension in your body, all the fears and worries, and then breathe them out, and let go of them. Take another deep breath and set yourself free.

Now just be still, be with Me and experience Me with you. No more words, no more thoughts, no more prayers. Just be with me and my Unconditional Love for you that is greater than everything you've told me.

Just "be" now, rest... your mind... your body... your emotions and spirit. Peace... finally peace!

Now you can do something for Me. Don't leave Me here. Take me with you, because that's where I will be. Stay aware that I am with you where ever you go. So let's go and enjoy the rest of the day together. Now our adventure begins!

DELIVERANCE RITUALS

Unfortunately, many Christians do not know they have been given the power and means to deliver themselves and others from attacks and temptations from Satan, Evil Spirits, and Powers.

"Deliver us from Evil"... (Mt. 6:13)

*"These are the signs that will follow **all believers... They will cast out devils.**"*
(Mk. 16:17-20)

Because many have not been taught this, they are either afraid of Satan and Evil, or they deny his existence. That's why Evil keeps winning, because there are fewer and fewer believers who oppose, attack, and cast them out.

Finally, you have the answer from Jesus, but not only the answer, but what to do and how to do it. The following are rituals that will enable you to use the power of the Lord to start winning and torture the Evil torturers that brought Sin, Suffering and Death into the world to us and our loved ones.

IMPORTANT: When using any of these rituals, you need to apply an "attitude." Do NOT show any signs of FEAR, no matter what you see, hear or feel. It's OK to be startled, but immediately respond by focusing on Jesus with you, then get in there and attack. When you are done attacking, attack again. And punish them with the name and blood of Jesus until they leave. The more you do it, the easier it gets, and they will be afraid of you, instead of you them. REMEMBER, don't be looking for Evil in everybody or everywhere. Keep your focus on the Lord and His Will. Oh yea, and enjoy life!

#1 A "CARRY WITH YOU" PRAYER FOR DELIVERANCE (short)

Jesus, bind and cast out whoever and whatever this is in Your name, and by the blood You shed on the Cross. Blessed Mother and St. Michael the Archangel, defend me and my loved ones. Satan and all Evil **Be Gone**, for I am a child of God. Amen!

#2 A RITUAL FOR DELIVERANCE

(For minor attacks of oppression)

In your name, Jesus, and by the blood You shed on the cross, the

Power and authority of the Holy Spirit, and through the intercession of you, Blessed Mother and St. Michael the Archangel, **I bind you, Satan, and all evil spirits and powers and command you to leave. I bind and cast you out and command you to go before the throne of God to do with you as He wills.**

Lord, grant me the grace to keep my attention on You here with me and not take back these lies by thinking about or dwelling on them.

I am a child of God. I belong to You, Jesus, and You alone. You are the Lord of my life. **Into Your hands, I commend my spirit.**

Response: **"Deliver me, Lord"**

<u>**FROM**</u>:

Fear and Anger...	*"Deliver me, Lord"*
Pride and Self-Righteousness...	*"Deliver me, Lord"*
Greed and Selfishness...	*"Deliver me, Lord"*
Envy and Jealousy...	*"Deliver me, Lord"*
Lust and Desires of the Flesh...	*"Deliver me, Lord"*
Hatred and Judging...	*"Deliver me, Lord"*
Depression and Loneliness...	*"Deliver me, Lord"*
Doubt and Despair...	*"Deliver me, Lord"*
Self-Hatred...	*"Deliver me, Lord"*

Replacing You, Lord, and my church family with my own desire for things and doing only what I want, instead of your will...*"Deliver me, Lord"*

RENEWAL OF MY BAPTISMAL PROMISES

- ☐ I surrender my entire mind, body, and spirit to You, Jesus, my Lord and Savior, and no other.
- ☐ I refuse to be mastered by Sin and Evil.
- ☐ I bind and cast you out by my love for Jesus.
- ☐ I renounce you, Satan, and all of your empty promises.

- ☐ I refuse to be mastered by Sin and Evil.
- ☐ I bind and cast you out by my love for Jesus.

Our Father *who art in Heaven, hallowed be Thy name. Thy Kingdom come, Thy will be done, on Earth as it is in Heaven. Give me this day, my daily bread, and forgive me my trespasses as I forgive those who trespass against me. And lead me through temptation, and* **deliver me from Evil***. Amen.*

WHEN FINISHED:

Glory to You, my Creator and Father, and to my Lord and Friend, Jesus the Christ, and You, the Holy Spirit, the Unconditional Love and Wisdom of God as it was in the beginning, is now and ever shall be. AMEN.

If you are attacked again, you **attack** *and torture Evil**, whoever and whatever they are, with the above prayers until they leave. Then go and enjoy life, because the reason He gives us power over temptation and Evil is to have JOY, LIFE, and PEACE, so get to it!*

#3 A RITUAL OF DELIVERANCE- FULL VERSION

For those evil spirits and demons that require more prayer and fasting

"Be Gone, Satan"

PRAYER OF PROTECTION

In the name of Jesus Christ our Lord by the intercession of Mary, immaculate Virgin and mother of God, by St. Michael the Archangel, the Apostles, Martyrs and Saints, and by the authority of the Holy Catholic Church, we ask for your protection from all the wickedness, evil, and harm to our bodies, minds, and souls by Satan and all evil powers, rulers, principalities, demons and spirits. We are merely sinners that trust in your mercy and forgiveness to be your instruments to deliver .... from all the evil that is tormenting them. Grant us the wisdom of the Holy Spirit to guide us through and to the completion of your will to cast out all evil from .... We ask this in Your name, Jesus, your precious blood, and ask that it be poured over all of us with your protection, love, wisdom and power. Amen.

PRAYER OF PRAISE

(Shared and spontaneous praises of the Lord, invoking the Holy Spirit to be the guide, wisdom, and director of the deliverance are offered at this time. Those with the gift of tongues should use their gift, praising the Lord and asking for the power of the Holy Spirit.)

Prayer of confession and forgiveness

"Confess your sins, draw near to me, and I will deliver and set you free."

R: *Lord, forgive me.*

Lord, if I have:

- ☐ Spent less and less time with you and drifted away from my church family... *Lord forgive me!*
- ☐ Judged, gossiped, and hurt others. *R.*
- ☐ Lusted, watched pornography, used others sexually. *R.*
- ☐ Been in unhealthy relationships. *R.*
- ☐ Held grudges and wanted to hurt someone who hurt me. *R.*
- ☐ Been involved in any occult practices and rituals, or with people involved with these evil powers. *R.*
- ☐ Been selfish, greedy and not have not participated in service ministry for the poor, sick, and the marginalized. *R.*
- ☐ Allowed Evil to attach itself to my body, mind and spirit, because of the pleasure and the power it gave me. *R.*
- ☐ Abused alcohol, drugs, and prescription medications. *R.*
- ☐ Abused and been used by others. *R.*

Prayer for power of deliverance

Lord God, our Almighty Father, You who created us, and You our Lord and Friend, Jesus the Christ, as you gave to your holy apostles and disciples the power to cast out and trample Satan, serpents and evil spirits, grant to us now that same power and authority now as we deliver _____ from any and all evil. Amen.

Prayer of deliverance

R: *In the name of Jesus, I cast you out.*

- ☐ All powers, principalities, rulers from the kingdom of darkness... *In the name of Jesus, I cast you out.*
- ☐ The spirits in charge in this oppression, obsession, and infestation...*R.*
- ☐ Spirits and demons of fear and lies...*R.*
- ☐ Spirits and demons of lust, sex abuse and rape...*R.*
- ☐ Spirits and demons of violence and hatred...*R.*
- ☐ Spirits and demons of physical abuse...*R.*
- ☐ All demons, spirits, powers of addiction and disease that have a hold on _____'s body, mind, feelings and will...*R.*
- ☐ All contacts and participation in occult practices, rituals, curses, witchcraft, use of articles of darkness and evil...*R.*

*Hold a crucifix and sprinkle holy water in four directions. And in a commanding voice read the following:

I cast out every unclean spirit, every Satanic power, every attack of the powers of darkness, every legion and principality, in the name of my Lord Jesus Christ.

Jesus pour your blood on, torture and punish:

- ☐ Jemjasa, Azezal, all the original fallen angels and their cohorts
- ☐ All those who made their covenant of rebellion and death on Mt. Hermon
- ☐ All of them—their children with human women, the Nephilim, the giants, and Satan himself
- ☐ The fallen angels that desecrated, brought sin and death to us and all physical reality
- ☐ All the powers, rulers and false gods from ancient times until the present
- ☐ Babylonian evil demons and spirits that have sprung from there.
- ☐ Ahab: corrupt, deceiver, liar, and pathetic king

- Jezebel: you are no queen, but the mother of the occult, sorcery, witchcraft, curses, the dark arts. You are most vile, most ugly, and most empty of all God's creatures
- Leviathan: child of Satan, a beast, a monster, corrupt, pathetic, and cursed
- Nimrod: son of Satan, would be god, usurper of God's power, a loser, self- righteous, arrogant, filled with pride, a fake, corruptor of all those in power, condemned to hell, powerlessness for all eternity
- All the powers, principalities, rulers, demons and spirits of Babylon, Sumer, Akadia, Psodom and Ghemorrah
- All your heads and pierce your tongues with spears and chains

***Glory, praise and honor be to You**, Father, to you our Lord and Friend Jesus the Christ—You the power, wisdom, Unconditional Love of God and the Holy Spirit. Amen!*

The Holy Spirit burns you, Satan, all evil demons and spirits with the knowledge and truth of your future and eternal damnation

For all eternity you will dwell in darkness with no experience or hope of light that you betrayed and lost.

- For all eternity, you have lost your former state.
- For all eternity, you will experience pain, but your bodies will not die.
- For all eternity, you will be imprisoned in hell without hope.
- For all eternity you will experience no love, no power, no pleasure, and no light, only darkness and despair.
- For all eternity, you will live in chaos and destroy one another without end.
- For all eternity, you are damned, cursed, despised, and powerless.
- For all eternity, you will be tortured, tormented, experience all the horrific suffering you caused humanity from the beginning.
- For all eternity, you will never see or experience God or the light of divinity.
- You will lose all the divine knowledge that you infected humanity with.

- ☐ You will rot in the very evil you created and without escape.

May the Holy Spirit:

- ☐ Dispel your lies and deceit
- ☐ Deliver this person from all evil
- ☐ Chain your powers
- ☐ Bind your displays of tricks and antics
- ☐ Bind and cast you out
- ☐ Condemn you to hell
- ☐ Compel you to never come back, oppress or obsess this person
- ☐ Command you to never seduce or try to take hold of their consciousness, soul, mind, or body.
- ☐ Break all gates, links, and pathways to your hierarchy of evil from the least of your spirits to Satan yourself.
- ☐ Torture, punish, and cause the greatest pain and suffering to all evil that is present here with the blood of our Lord Jesus the Christ.

St. Michael the Archangel and all warrior angels:

- ☐ Punishes you evil ones
- ☐ Condemns you
- ☐ Pierces you with the sword of the truth
- ☐ Binds and casts you out
- ☐ Inflicts horrific suffering and pain on all of you
- ☐ Commands you to accept defeat and leave, or your punishment will continue.

Blessed Mother

Mother of our Lord and Savior Jesus the Christ, you who stood before the beast who was ready to devour your child, but you gave birth to the Son of God who conquered our fears, temptation, sin, and death itself. Destroy, bind, cast out, and deliver this child of God from all evil including the beast that Jesus, our Lord and Savior, condemned to the fires of hell.

Mary, Mother of God...

- ☐ Mary, Most Holy...*R.* Cast them out with the blood of your Son.
- ☐ Mary, Queen of Heaven...*R.*
- ☐ Mary, Our Lady of Victory...*R.*
- ☐ Mary, Our Lady of Peace...*R.*
- ☐ Mary, Most Powerful...*R.*
- ☐ Mary, Our Lady of Consolation...*R.*
- ☐ Mary, Our Mother...*R.*

All you Saints & Holy Ones

By the authority of the Church and all believers, deliver and punish Satan and Evil that is present here with the light of our faith and love for the Father, Son, and Holy Spirit.

- ☐ Light of St. Michael...*R.* Punishes and casts you out.
- ☐ Light of St. Francis...*R.*
- ☐ Light of St. Benedict...*R.*
- ☐ Light of St. Aloysius...*R.*
- ☐ Light of St. Peter...*R.*
- ☐ Light of St. James and John...*R.*
- ☐ Light of St. Paul and St. Andrew...*R.*
- ☐ Light of all the disciples...*R.*
- ☐ Light of St. Anthony...*R.*
- ☐ Light of St. Elizabeth Ann Seton...*R.*
- ☐ Light of St. Catherine...*R.*
- ☐ Light of St. John the XXIII...*R.*
- ☐ Light of St. John Paul II...*R.*
- ☐ Light of St. Marianne Kope...*R.*
- ☐ Light of St. Agnes and Agatha...*R.*
- ☐ Light of St. Clare...*R.*
- ☐ Light of St. Dominick...*R.*
- ☐ All the angels, martyrs, saints, powers and principalities of Heaven...*R.*
- ☐ The Holy Catholic Church and all of God's children...*R.*

THE TRUTH OF THE RESURRECTION CASTS YOU OUT

- ☐ The Resurrection destroyed your powers of fear, sin, and death.

- The Resurrection is now ours.
- The Resurrection will cause you the greatest torment.
- The Resurrection raises us to the heights of Heaven as the Father's children.
- The Resurrection will torment you now and forever with the knowledge that God has given to us what you never had and will never know or experience for all eternity.
- You who seduced and experimented with our physical bodies and minds and brought sin, suffering, and death into the world and us has now been undone by Christ's Resurrection.
- We will be re-created with new resurrected bodies in Heaven, and you will be left in hell forever with no more bodies to tempt, possess, or destroy.
- The Resurrection casts you out with the knowledge of what you lost and condemned yourselves for all eternity, and for lust and power. You are the most pathetic of all created beings.
- May the blood of Christ and His Resurrection deliver your influence, hold, and attachment not only to ____ who belongs to God, but back to 10 generations in her/his family.
- The blood of Christ and His Resurrection breaks and destroys all bonds, legal rights and holds on mind, body and soul, back to 10 generations.
- Your time here, Satan, is over. We will continue to torture you until you leave.

Therefore, in the name of You, our Lord Jesus the Christ right here with us, by his most precious blood, the Holy Spirit, and the power of God our Almighty Father, every unclean spirit, every legion, every diabolical group or sect, be bound, delivered, and cast out.

In their place, Lord, grant our sister/brother peace, Unconditional Love, and fill them with the Holy Spirit as we renew our baptismal promises, renouncing Satan, all evil, and profess our faith and love for you, Father, Son, and Holy Spirit.

RENEWAL OF OUR BAPTISMAL PROMISES

Together with _____ let us renew the promises of our Holy Baptism, when we renounced Satan and his works and promised to serve God in the Holy Catholic Church.

And so I ask you:

V. Do we renounce you, Satan?
R. We do.

V. And all your works.
R. We do.

V. And all of your empty promises.
R. We do.

V. Do we renounce sin, so as to live in the freedom of the children of God.
R. We do.

V. Do we renounce the lure of evil, so that sin may have no mastery over us?
R. We do.

V. Do we renounce Satan, the author and prince of sin?
R. We do.

V. Do we believe in God, the Father Almighty, Creator of Heaven and Earth?
R. We do.

V. Do we believe in Jesus Christ, his only Son, our Lord who was born of the Virgin Mary, suffered death, was buried, rose again from the dead, and is seated at the right hand of the Father?
R. We do.

V. Do we believe in the Holy Spirit, the Holy Catholic Church, the communion of saints, the forgiveness of sins, the resurrection of the body, and life everlasting?
R. We do.

May you Almighty God, the Father of our Lord Jesus Christ, who has given us new birth by water and the Holy Spirit and bestowed on us forgiveness of our sins, deliver us from Satan and all evil by his grace and blood.
R. Amen.

OUR FATHER WHO ART IN HEAVEN... (Sprinkle all with holy water)

May you, the Almighty God bless, watch over and protect _____, his/her house, family, and all of us, in the name of the Father, Son and Holy Spirit. Amen.

TWO GREAT GIFTS FROM GOD FOR HEALING

*Now that I am an "old goat" and ministered to thousands of people for 45 years, I have learned that the Lord gave all of us two incredible Gifts to deal with Suffering.

The Lord has given us two great gifts. Both of these need to be developed and experienced. One gift has the power of God to deliver us from fear, worry, anger, grief, sadness, depression, and even despair. The other helps put all of our problems and suffering that overwhelm us into perspective and lifts us out of them to a "freedom zone" of elation and joy, which we thought were impossible.

What are these two wonderful gifts that the Lord has given us? **TEARS & LAUGHTER**!

TEARS, CRYING, EVEN WAILING will turn into a volcano eruption, finally releasing the pressure and darkness of Fear, Worry, Stress, Loneliness. When we stop crying, there is peace and rest. The flames of suffering cool down until they build up again. But we remain in gratitude for peace to come.

LAUGHTER. I mean a good belly laugh, when you feel like your chest is going to explode, and you can't stop *(I hope you have experienced at least one)*. If you have had the laugh in the middle of a disaster, or a really, really, BAD day, then you know what I mean.

Laughter lifts us up from the temptation of despair and thinking that it can't get any worse. Laughter, at that moment, catapults us magically and miraculously into another zone filled with joy, elation, and hope. When we finally stop laughing, we receive the truth and realization that it's not the **END OF THE WORLD**. As the Lord and the Word of God says, **It came to Pass.**

The Lord has taught me that laughing together in the ZONE **is** REALITY and **NOT** life here in these earthly bodies subject to Sin, Suffering, and Death.

Laughter is a taste of "Heaven"

JESUS: "FOR MY YOUNG TEENAGERS"

"There's another Way"

Teenagers and young people who come to me over the years tell me of the things they struggle with and cause a great deal of confusion, pain, and unhappiness.

- Not fitting in at school, feeling excluded by so many cliques
- Being made fun of with what I look like and what I don't look like
- Laughed at because of what I did and what I couldn't do
- Gossiped about and my reputation destroyed
- Feeling like everybody was judging me
- Coming from a broken home and feeling lonely
- Feeling like I don't know how to do anything
- Being touched, groped and sexually abused
- Sexual confusion. Am I gay or straight? I feel I can't tell anybody, not even my parents. I'll be rejected and even attacked if I do\

JESUS:

"Anyone who leads one of these little ones astray, it would be better if a millstone were put around their neck and cast into the sea." (Lk. 17:2)

Jesus is perfectly clear about His love for teenagers and children. When it comes to teenagers, I am convinced that Evil has seduced young people today with electronics, cell phones, sports, gaming, sex, alcohol and drugs. In terms of Jesus, faith, and church, we have lost two generations, and that includes many of their parents. The real tragedy is that Evil has not only seduced young people today but has manipulated them into addiction. If you don't believe that, take a cell phone from a teenager and note their reaction.

Like all addictions, they only get worse and lead to destruction and death. They have become slaves to their desires, which are insatiable. They require more of everything, and there is never enough. I am sure I don't need to add anything further as I'm sure it's quite apparent to you, the reader, what is happening in our country and around the world with young people.

GOOD NEWS: Over the years I have given hundreds of retreats for teenagers and have listened carefully to their stories of emptiness, boredom, dissatisfaction, and scars from their choices and actions. In recent years I find that teens and young adults are getting tired of the unfulfilled promises that their addictions have left them with. It has left them with emptiness and dissatisfaction plus the pain from others.

They are hungry for "another Way" but don't believe there is. The GOOD NEWS is that when teens today are revealed another Way, they are not only curious but open to it. When I introduce Jesus as someone who is God and not just what old people believe in and go to church for, they express a real desire to learn about and experience this being who loves them.

After I witness to them, I teach them how to talk to Jesus and have a personal relationship with Him as friends. I pray with them to Jesus, and then pray over them to receive the Holy Spirit whenever the Lord thinks they are ready.

More and more teens who really want to know that there is another way to think and live, choose to ask, seek, and knock for Jesus to open the door and enter their lives with the Holy Spirit. I am blessed to witness to hundreds of young people when they did experience the Holy Spirit and are now on Fire in a friendship relationship with Jesus. Their awesome love for Jesus and commitment to do His will inspires me to grow in my love for the Lord.

So if you are a teenager or young adult, and you're tired of being bored and dissatisfied with everything you've been doing, scarred by your choices and actions, then I have included the following prayers for you. **TIME WITH JESUS** is when you are feeling down by your problems. Read it and listen to Jesus calm you by His Unconditional Love for you. **TEENS PRAYER TO JESUS** is when you really want to know and experience the Holy Spirit, just as you experience the presence of your best friend.

Just remember, it's not magic, just like it wasn't magic when you started any friendship. You didn't become friends over night. Just keep using this prayer to ask Jesus for the Holy Spirit, whether you experience Him or not. When He knows you are really sincere and ready, YOU WILL.

SOMETHING IS MISSING

(from the diary of a teenage girl)

One of the hardest parts of being a teenager is that I felt I didn't know where I fit in or who I was supposed to be.

One night when I began to pray to Jesus on the cross, it was then that I felt a real presence come to me and knew it was really Him. I felt God's love right inside me and the experience is hard to describe. I prayed thousands of time before, but never felt much of anything, because I never believed I could, but this time I really believed I could, and wanted to know Jesus was there and cared about me. Well, He really was there, and I felt Him with me. I wish every teenager could experience Jesus. You can, if you only keep asking, and when He thinks you are ready, you will." Megan (teen from Buffalo, NY)

ERIN'S WITNESS:

Jesus helps me with my every day decisions in life. He is part of my thoughts, and He shows me how to live my life. All I know is that when I do the things He asks me to, it feels great, better than any high I get from soccer, and I love soccer. (Erin, teenager from Denver, CO)

JESUS SPEAKS TO YOU, TEENS

#1 TEENS "TIME WITH JESUS" PRAYER

(When you have problems, feel alone, hurt, and stressed— listen to Jesus.)

SLOW DOWN. *Take a Time Out. It's me, Jesus, your Lord and your Friend. I've been waiting for you...waiting for you to spend time with me...just you and Me...*
I know there's a lot of things going through that mind of yours; new problems to solve, people that hurt you and wondering if you'll always feel this way.

So take time out and stay right here with Me. Stop trying to fix your problems by yourself or ignore them by spending time on your cell phone, texting, computer games, sports or being busy all the time. The minute you stop doing these things, you are bored, unhappy and the problems remain.

You see, thinking about your problems over and over is what's causing your worry, loneliness, and pain. Relax, take a break and stop letting them beat you up.

Take your time now, and tell me what's bothering you and stressing you out. Tell me... let go of it...and let me take care of it...

Tell me if what's bothering you is feeling guilty for anything you have done, anything you are ashamed of or hate yourself for. There is no need to feel this way! Just tell me what you did, ask for forgiveness and a new start, and it will be yours. I not only will forgive you if you ask, but more importantly, I want you to know and experience that I love you any way. My love for you is greater than anything you did. So take time now, and tell me your sins, so I can set you free.

Remember, don't let your sins keep you away from me and drag you down to hate yourself. Always talk to me, and let go of them. Your goodness does not come from you being perfect. It comes from you experiencing that I love you anyway, and the more you experience my love throughout your day, the less you will sin.

Now, no more words, no more thoughts, no more prayers. Just be still, rest, and enjoy being with me, safe, without worry. Just relax in peace, finally peace...

Close your eyes and just be still. Imagine that I am right there with you, because I am. Take as much time as you need.

Then open your eyes.

Lastly, don't leave Me here. Take me with you, by being aware that I am with you. So let's go and experience the rest of this day together. C'mon, let's go.

#2 TEENS' DAILY PRAYER

Jesus, I want to know you more and really experience all the love you had for me on the Cross. I want you to become my Friend. I want to be yours.

I want to be more aware of you with me throughout my day, talk to you, and be able to tell you anything.

I want you to not only help me with my problems, but teach me how to live and become a better person. Until then, I will try to take time throughout my day to talk to you and be aware that the Holy Spirit, Your Unconditional Love for me, is right there with me as you are now. Jesus, increase my faith and help me to be your Friend. Amen!

CHAPTER 17: COMMENCEMENT

Well, there you have it! I am finished with my part co-authoring this book. My intention was to give Jesus an opportunity to answer many of your questions about your life, teach you what to do about them, and how to do it.

I prayed continually to the Holy Spirit to give me wisdom, and I prayed to the Lord to reveal the WHAT TO DOs and HOW TO DO ITs. From beginning to end, I asked Jesus to keep my thoughts and interpretations separate from His Truth, and most of all, to keep my EGO out of it. I leave it up to you to decide if it was successful for you. Lastly, I want to say a prayer to the Lord for you.

MY PRAYER FOR YOU

Jesus, I pray that you have used this book to personally speak to its reader. I pray that they will experience Your Unconditional Love and Baptism with the Holy Spirit, if they have not already. Mostly, I pray that they will grow in Unconditional Love, Forgiveness, Generosity and be healed and delivered from their fears and worry. I pray they will find peace in the knowledge that wherever they are in faith, they have been taught that the God who created them, loves them and always has and always will. **AMEN!**

P.S. Every once in a while, read the questions in the Introduction. See if you can remember the answers, but more importantly, are you living them?

As my Baptist Preacher friend, Ernie, always said,

"Who knows what ya gonna do when the Holy Ghost gets inside Ya!"

THE END

or

COMMENCEMENT

> "Now C'mon, follow Me. And don't leave me here in this book!"
> *Jesus*

AUTHOR

Jesus

> I am a Franciscan friar of Holy Name Province, NY.
>
> That's all you need to know about me.
>
> I encourage you to read about the Author in the New Testament.

CO-AUTHOR

Fr. Francis Pompei ofm

REFERENCES

Andrus, Ralph. "BUSY." Satan's Meeting, 2007. www.sermons. faithlife.com/sermons/17736-satan%27s-meeting

Cohen, M. J. (1997) *RECONNECTING WITH NATURE: Finding wellness through restoring your bond with the Earth. Ecopress, Corvallis, WA.*

Johnson, Ken. (2012) Ancient Book of Enoch. CreateSpace Independent Publishing Platform.

Nelson, Thomas. *God's Promises & Answers for Your Life.* W. Publishing, Inc., 1995 & J. Countryman, a division of Thomas Nelson, Inc. Nashville, TN, 1999.

New International Version of the New American Bible (Old and New Testaments)

Wilson, Edward. O. *The Diversity of Life.* Cambridge: Harvard University Press, 1992.

BOOKS HIGHLY RECOMMENDED *because of their inspiration, influence on me, and because they are written by authors experiencing Jesus & the Holy Spirit.*

Embraced By The Light   *by Betty Eadie*

Jesus Calling   *by Sarah Young*

Proof Of Heaven   *by Dr. Eben Alexander*

HOW THE COVER PICTURE CAME TO BE

Mary Jo Woyciesjes was a 16 year old student who attended Bishop Grimes High School in Syracuse, New York, in 1976.

In the course of a weekend school retreat, Mary Jo experienced deeply, the love of the Lord in her heart.

In only a few short days, Mary Jo, with only a pen and an art pad, created what you are looking at. It is truly from the spirit of a teenager's faith. I know, because I was her teacher and Mary Jo gave it to me, and I have gazed upon it for many years.

Not to draw attention to her name and distract from Jesus' countenance, she wove her name into the drawing. Can you find it?

Thousands of people have written letters telling of how, while looking at this picture, were brought to tears and experienced the healing presence of Jesus.

CPSIA information can be obtained
at www.ICGtesting.com
Printed in the USA
BVHW030215081019
560445BV00002BA/207/P